RESPONDING
TO
GOD'S CALL

A Survival Guide

Roslyn A. Karaban

Resource Publications, Inc.
San Jose, California

Reprint Department
Resource Publications, Inc.
160 E. Virginia Street #290
San Jose, CA 95112-5876
(408) 286-8505 (voice)
(408) 287-8748 (fax)

Library of Congress Cataloging-in-Publication Data
Karaban, Roslyn A.
   Responding to God's Call : a survival guide / Roslyn A. Karaban.
      p.   cm.
   Includes bibliographical references.
   ISBN 0-89390-431-7 (pbk.)
   1. Vocation, Ecclesiastical—Psychology. 2. Grief—Religious aspects—Catholic Church. I. Title.
BX2380.K37   1997
248.8'9—dc21   97-48829
                                           CIP

Printed in the United States of America.
02 01 00 99 98 | 5 4 3 2 1

Editorial director: Nick Wagner
Project coordinator: Mike Sagara
Production assistant: David Dunlap

Author photograph by Leichtner Studios, Inc.

To my children,
Deepa and Micah Premnath:
May they benefit from my difficulties.

Contents

Acknowledgments

This work represents a *lifetime* of discernment and grieving yet was written in only the last two years of my life. This was possible because of:

- Patricia Schoelles, SSJ, President of St. Bernard's Institute, who invited me to give a faculty lecture in March 1994. That lecture, "Responding to Call: Working through Grief," became the basis for this book.

- my students and clients and friends who have privileged me with their stories of discernment and grieving. Particular thanks go to the students from my "Self-Discernment in Ministry" classes.

- my editor, Nick Wagner, who continues to diligently, faithfully, and cheerfully guide me through the arduous process of writing. This book has benefited greatly from his careful editing.

- my readers, Herbert Anderson of Catholic Theological Union in Chicago; Robert Wicks of Loyola College in Maryland; Han van den Blink of Colgate Rochester Divinity School; and Leigh Sutcliffe Ramsey of Colgate Rochester Divinity School. Their feedback has strengthened the content of this book and their encouragement has sustained me in my writing.

- Peter Beisheim of Stonehill College, my mentor and guide from college days and beyond, who was the first to affirm my call and who continues to support me in my ministry.

- my endorser, Robert J. Wicks, who has uplifted me with his kind words.

- my colleagues who served as resources in my writing, especially Robert Kennedy of St. Bernard's Institute.

- the staff of Ambrose Swasey Library at Colgate Rochester Divinity School, especially Thomas Haverly and Kayt Huttlin, who responded to my many requests with patience and kindness.

- the production staff at Resource Publications, Inc., who put the finishing touches on this book.

- my family and friends, who put up with me and encouraged me through the writing process, especially my husband, Devadasan Premnath, and my best friend, Nancy Stetson Wrobel.

Finally, I wish to note that some of the material for this book came from talks I have given in the last two years. Besides the talk in March 1994 which formed the basis for this book, much of my material on grieving was put together for a talk given at Colgate Rochester Divinity School/St. Bernard's Institute in March 1996: "Grief: Personal, Pastoral and Prophetic Considerations." Much of my material on spirituality was gathered for a talk given in February 1996 for St. Bernard's on the Road: "Living a Spiritual Life in a Busy World."

in the United States of America, and are used by permission. All rights reserved.

Excerpted from *Seeds of Sensitivity* by Robert J. Wicks. Copyright 1995 by Ave Maria Press, Notre Dame, IN 46556. Used with permission of the publisher.

From *The Book of Discipline of The United Methodist Church—1998*. Copyright © 1988 by the United Methodist Publishing House. Used by permission.

From *Discernment: A Study in Ecstasy and Evil* by Morton Kelsey. Copyright © 1978 by Paulist Press. Used by permission of Paulist Press.

From *By Way of the Heart* by W. Au. Copyright © 1989 by Paulist Press. Used by permission of Paulist Press.

From *Women at the Well: Feminist Perspectives on Spiritual Direction* by K. Fisher. Copyright © 1988 by Paulist Press. Used by permission of Paulist Press.

From *LIVING BEYOND LOSS: Death in the Family* by Froma Walsh and Monica McGoldrick, editors. Copyright © 1991 by Froma Walsh and Monica McGoldrick. Reprinted by permission of W. W. Norton & Company, Inc.

In the event that some source or copyright holder has been overlooked, please send acknowledgment requirements to the editorial director at Resource Publications, Inc.

Introduction

Very often the concept of "call" has been associated with ordained or professional (ecclesial) ministry. As Christians we are *all* called to be part of God's vision. God offers us this invitation in Scripture and through our continuing relationship with God as a Christian people. In Scripture we find both a very broad call to share in God's life as well as very specific stories of call.[1] The broad call to ministry in Scripture includes all who are called into relationship with God. Today, we live in an "age of discernment" when "every Christian [is called] to a responsible, prophetic role in living and proclaiming the faith" (Green 11).

We receive God's call in *baptism*, when we become new creations in Christ—who is priest, prophet, and king ("Rite of Baptism for Several Children" 62). Thus, as baptized Christians we are *all called* to live out and proclaim our faith as we promise to "remain for ever a member of Christ."[2] Our baptismal promises unite us with a community of faith with a common purpose: to be faithful followers of Christ and witnesses to his Gospel (RBSC 47).[3]

How we are called to live out the Gospel will differ from person to person, for in addition to God's call to all of us,

1

God calls each one of us in different ways. It is up to each one of us to *discern* how our piece of the vision relates to God's vision. Walter Brueggemann describes God's vision in this way:

> The central vision of world history in the Bible is that all of creation is one....Israel has a vision of all persons being drawn into a single community (Acts 2:11)....The most staggering expression of the vision is that all persons are *children of a single family*...and bearers of a single destiny, namely, the care and management of all of God's creation.
>
> That persistent vision of joy, well-being, harmony, and prosperity is not captured in any single word or idea in the Bible, and a cluster of words is required to express its many dimensions and subtle nuances: love, loyalty, truth, grace, salvation, justice, blessing, right-eousness...*shalom* (*Living Toward a Vision* 15-16).

In addition to seeing how our piece of the vision relates to God's vision, we need to discern our particular *call*. Our faith is our personal awakening and response to this call (Finley 19). In discerning our call it is first necessary to understand how vision is different from call. "Vision is seeing the big picture; call is the way we can implement the vision in a particular time and place" (McMakin and Nary 203). We discover "glimmers" of God's vision in reflection and prayer when we discover that which "evokes our most passionate criticism, our deepest grief, or energizes us to new possibilities" (204).

Thus, call is the particular way we implement what we understand our piece of God's vision to be.

My story of glimpsing God's vision and discerning God's call is a story of a vision of inclusivity and equality and a call to implement that vision through priesthood. I believe my glimpse of God's vision is part of God's greater story as revealed to us in Scripture, tradition, and personal experience. William Bausch describes a sixfold process for discernment that begins with understanding that our own personal story is part of God's greater story (203-204). "The call to ministry begins as a story; a story of an encounter between an individual and God" (Myers 7). I have used Bausch's schema (203-209) as a model for my own discernment and for guiding others in their discernment process:

1. Learn the story: the larger story of God's revelation and the smaller story of our own personal history.

2. Own our story: accept the good and the bad in our life.

3. Contemplate the story.

4. Pray the story.

5. Share the story:
   a. with a confidant,
   b. through witnessing, evangelizing and teaching, and
   c. by tapping into the needs of the poor and oppressed as an advocate of social justice.

6. Share the story by being part of a larger worshiping and witnessing community.

This book describes another sixfold process of discernment—not as a replacement of Bausch's model or other models of discernment but as an addition to these schemas written from my own particular glimpse of the vision and experience of call. I begin this book with my story of call as one example of discernment. I begin with my own story because it is most familiar to me and because I have discovered in my own story certain obstacles and complications that are common to other stories of call and discernment. If recognized and named, these obstacles can be gotten through and discernment can be more fully realized. Furthermore, I have discovered that, by understanding that the discernment process and grieving process are irrevocably linked, discerners will be able to heal and grow. It is my hope that these discoveries will serve as aids to discerners and to those who guide discerners.

Prelude

My Story of Call: A Case Study in Grieving

The story[1] of my call begins with my call to the ordained priesthood when I was eight years old. I lived in a small town where there were two churches: one Roman Catholic, one Protestant. As a Catholic, I was not allowed to know anything about the Protestant church. However, I was also a Brownie Scout and we held our meetings in the basement of the Protestant church. One day we did not meet in the basement but went outside to do something—no doubt to work toward one of the many badges we were encouraged to earn. One of the girls I was with suggested that we go up the outer stairs of the church and look inside. Although I feared we would be breaking some sort of law—religious, if not legal—curiosity and peer pressure convinced me to take a peek. I don't remember much of what I saw when I looked in, but I do remember what one of the girls *told* me about the church. She said that the minister's wife helped the

5

minister in the church. I didn't hear much else. I got caught on the revelation that ministers could have wives.

I was already feeling that God was calling me to ministry within the church, but I kept pushing this idea aside. I couldn't get a clear picture of what God was calling me to do, but even then I knew God was not calling me to be a nun. The news that ministers could have wives excited me, and a new possibility emerged for me. Maybe I could still be a Roman Catholic female, but I could *marry* a Protestant minister and help *him* in his ministry. I was comforted by this, and I was able for a while to put aside any other options.

Many years later, I did marry a Protestant minister, although my reasons for doing so had changed. I did not marry him to help him in *his* ministry. I had become painfully aware that my call was not to be the *wife* of someone who was ordained but to be ordained myself.

In the beginning, then, I did not understand what God was asking of me. The attitude toward women in society and church, and my own acceptance of these attitudes, were strong enough to prevent me from developing my own sense of what my call was until I reached college. It was there that I came to know and understand that my call was to become a priest. Because that was not possible, I compromised by majoring in religious studies so that I could become a teacher of religious studies.

I was surprised when I realized I was called to be a priest—and then relieved. After all those years of trying to understand what I was called to do, discerning that it was to be a priest was like finding a lost piece of a puzzle and for the first time seeing a complete picture. There was a sense of wholeness, peace, joy, and achievement. These feelings were soon overshadowed, however, by the reality of what living out my call meant.

At first I had great hopes that the church would change, accept my call, and ordain me. This may sound very naive, but I was young. The church was making rapid changes in the wake of Vatican II. However, as the days, weeks, months, and then years continued to roll by without change, my joy diminished and my disbelief grew. As I continued to face an unchanging and uncompromising church, at least in regard to the ordination of women, I began to doubt my call. I found myself asking: "Do you really mean me, Lord? Are you sure you have the right person? Maybe if I teach religious studies, I can serve you. Did I misunderstand you? Did *you* miss something here? I am a female and a Roman Catholic. How can you be calling *me* to the priesthood?"

Although I would not have named it as such then, I can now see that I was experiencing one of the first "stages" of grief[2]—the stage of shock and disbelief. I continue to go through that first stage over and over again as I experience the dissonance[3] between the clear experience of my call and the denial by the institutional church that my call exists.[4] However, there came a time when I could no longer deny what I believed God was calling me to do. I then moved into feelings of loneliness, sadness, fear and anxiety—mostly about my future. If I was called by God to become a priest, what did this mean? At twenty-one I was willing to give up home, security, friends, and even the possibility of marriage, but I was not willing to give up my Roman Catholic faith tradition. I knew that joining a Protestant denomination would make ordination possible, but God was not asking this of me.

The only thing that got me through that time of confusion and despondency was a loving and wise mentor[5] who both supported me and guided me. To this day, I continue to give thanks to God for him. I was not aware at the time that I was grieving, or more precisely that I needed to grieve, but I now believe that that is what was happening. Because I was not aware that I was grieving, nor did I name it as such, I continued to work through my grief quite by chance.

With the encouragement of my mentor, I went on to study at a Protestant seminary to prepare for ministry. At that time it was not yet common for Roman Catholic seminaries to accept female students. At this seminary I was surrounded by women and men, most of whom were preparing for ordained ministry in a variety of denominations. It was there that I came most in touch with the feeling of *anger* that I was experiencing, and it was this anger that carried me through most of my Master of Divinity studies. I found myself asking, "Why can't I live out my call when my classmates can live out theirs? What is wrong with me? What is wrong with the Roman Catholic church? Why do I stay?"

Throughout all of this I thought that I had accepted my call. I can now see that I was working through what an understanding of accepting that call would mean. I now believe that accepting my call means accepting my anger and pain but also moving through and beyond these feelings (see Postlude). I tried to remain open to different possibilities, and I even considered joining the Episcopal church.

One of my most painful junctures came after I spent a summer serving as a Roman Catholic student minister in a national park. I faced both acceptance and rejection of me as minister because of my gender. I came back to my third year at seminary with a realization that there was not a place for me in parish ministry in the Roman Catholic Church. There was not yet the wide variety of ministries open to laity, and there was certainly no position comparable to pastoral associate or pastoral administrator, which I would have been very happy doing. And so the way I dealt with my pain was to put off making a decision about how to live out my call to the priesthood by going on for further studies. I lived by the maxim, "When in doubt, keep going to school."

In doing so, however, I kept myself stuck in a cycle of denial, anger, bargaining, and depression.[6] I did not identify my experiences as grieving. I was unable to move through these emotions to resolution, reconnection, and what I would call resurrection. I thank God that I had people who could minister to me throughout all of this, although we didn't know what to call what I was going through. For it was in graduate school that I discovered that I was not *alone* in my experience. I was not the only confused, despondent, angry, hopeful, called, and grieving Roman Catholic woman. Connecting to others like me with similar experiences and feelings was my saving grace. It was also the beginning of being able to work through my denial, to express and work through my feelings, and to get through my grieving.[7] Or so I thought.

While working through these feelings, I found what I thought to be an "alternative ministry" of pastoral counseling. I had begun this shift in my third year of seminary and decided to continue this alternate path in graduate school. That way, I could sidestep and even avoid the issue of ordination while still pursuing and preparing for a ministry of pastoral counseling. What I didn't realize, however, was that in the field of pastoral counseling, it was assumed that a pastoral counselor is an ordained minister or priest who did advanced training in counseling theory and skills. Yet here I was working as a pastoral counselor in a pastoral counseling center and studying for a degree in pastoral counseling. Once again I experienced the feeling of cognitive dissonance, like there must be something wrong with *me*. At this time there was no place in the field of pastoral counseling for lay pastoral counselors, Roman Catholic or Protestant, even if we were theologically trained and called to be there. I discovered that the alternative was to *teach* pastoral counseling. I was back to the compromise I had made in college—having to consider teaching as the way to live out my call to ministry.

This was all too much for me, and I gave up—not on life but on my call to ministry. I did this by moving twelve thousand miles in order to get away from my pain. The redeeming news was that I was no longer in denial, nor was I confused. I had reached a point of apathy about ordained ministry in the Roman Catholic Church and decided to leave these concerns for others to worry about and work toward. I was tired and desired to live a "normal" life. I married, finished my PhD, had my first child, and left the United States to go live in India, where my husband (the Protestant minister) would be teaching full-time in a Protestant seminary. As part of my farewell gift to the Roman

Catholic Church, my call, and my grieving, I left behind a doctoral dissertation for the next generation—my daughter—saying in my dedication: "May she benefit from my struggles" ("Pastoral Counselor: Role or Function?"). I believed, or at least hoped, that my struggles and my grieving were over. I had poured out my pain in my thesis, presenting a new, alternative, lay model for Roman Catholic pastoral counseling, assuming that others would continue to fight the battle. I had done my part.

Part I

How Do We Know God Is Calling Us?

Chapter One

Experience the Call

God's call to *each* of us is an *invitation* that we need to hear, understand, and respond to. This chapter focuses on the necessity to *hear* and *experience* God's call in each of our lives. We will be better able to do this if we first understand some basic characteristics of call.

There is no one way or right way to experience God's call in our lives.

In my own life, I have experienced God's call as both specific and concrete as well as dramatic and "cataclysmic" (Myers 71)—as both "the voice of one crying out in the wilderness" (Mt 3:3a, NRSV) and as part of my everyday living and interacting with others. I have experienced God's call as clear and evocative and as a vague and gentle tugging at my heart. When the call has been specific or cataclysmic, it has been harder to ignore. When the call has been more of a longing or a gentle tugging, it has been easier to put off until the gentle tugging has become a strong pull. I found, however, in putting off a response to God's call, I have become increasingly restless, dissatisfied, uncomfortable, uneasy, and expectant, waiting for something (I knew not what) to happen, to relieve me of my feelings.

I have also found that we can ask to be called, but we cannot make it happen; call comes to us and we must listen and wait (Finley 29).

I used to believe that everyone who went into ministry—particularly ordained or professional ministry—received a specific and very clear message from God. Through my work in teaching and guiding others in their discernment process and listening to the stories of my clients and students, I have come to understand otherwise. For some of us, the call is general, even vague. Dag Hammarskjöld, former Secretary of the United Nations, wrote of "call" in this way:

> I don't know Who—or what—put the question. I don't know when it was put. I don't even remember answering. But at some moment I did answer *Yes* to Someone—or Something—and from that hour I was certain that existence is meaningful and that, therefore, my life, in self-surrender, had a goal (205).

For others, the call is general but clearer. It is experienced as a gradual understanding of God's purpose, a growing sense of inner direction; it is experienced as subtle or unmistakable (Farnham et al. 7). We experience signs of this more subtle or gradual sense as a feeling of restlessness, of dissatisfaction, of being at a crossroads, that something is happening, of transition, of being drawn, or of yearning and wondering (11).

This is the way Joan[1] experienced her call to ministry. She did not hear particular words from God, nor did she experience any other sensory phenomena often associated with call, such as a bright light. Yet she has experienced a nudging toward ministry, a desire to help others, to serve, and to do ministry. And she has been told by others that she would make a good (ordained) minister. Joan has still not decided if she believes that God is calling her to priesthood. However, she is, after many years, trying to decide what the tuggings in her heart mean and what to do about them. Joan has actively and knowingly entered into a process of discernment.

Some of us, on the other hand, do experience very particular, unmistakable calls to ministry and do experience a sensory phenomena such as a bright light, voice, or a vision of Christ. Linda is one of these people. Linda was walking down the street one day when she heard God say to her, "You are to become a minister and serve me and my people all the days of your life." For her, it was that clear and that vivid, and she has lived her life from that day in response to that specific call.

William Myers interviewed eighty-six men and women from ten different Protestant, African-American church traditions across the United States. He found that there were three ways call to ministry was experienced (71-73):

- **Type A: Cataclysmic/Reluctant**—The experience of call was a momentous event, and the response was one of reluctance, that this was not what the callee wanted or expected; sanction from the community was secondary to the cataclysmic call experience itself, much like the experience of the apostle Paul.

- **Type B: Noncataclysmic/Reluctant**—The sense of call unfolded gradually; there were no cataclysmic moments or turning points; still, there was reluctance, even resistance, in response to gradual awareness; sanction took the form of a series of events and the community of faith helped in recognizing the call.

- **Type C: Noncataclysmic/Nonreluctant**—Early religious exposure was critical; the callee was willing and was groomed and nurtured for ministry throughout his or her life; struggle with the call and search for sanction was non-existent, much like the calls of Isaiah and Timothy.

In hearing and reading the stories of call from my students, I would add a fourth category to Myers' three:

- **Type D: Cataclysmic/Nonreluctant**—The call involves a cataclysmic event, and this experience remains primary; the response is one of nonresistance, even acceptance; seeking sanction from the community is secondary but when sought may be blocked (see chapter five).

The two examples I have cited (Joan and Linda) focus on a call to ordained or professional ministry. Those who feel called to professional ministry have actually experienced at least four dimensions to their call (Aleshire 23):[2]

1. call to be a Christian—no pastoral minister has a call to ministry without first experiencing a call to be a Christian;

2. secret call—an inner experience or perception of a call to ministry;

18

3. providential call—a reception of gifts necessary to do ministry;

4. ecclesiastical call—an affirmation from a church community.

I will explore each dimension of this type of call to ministry further. However, this is not the only type of call.

We experience call in numerous ways to do various things. We are each uniquely gifted by God, and God calls each one of us. "God chose you from the beginning" (2 Thess 2:13b RSV).

Thomas has not experienced a call to professional or ordained ministry, but he has experienced God's call in his life. He has been working with a spiritual director (guide) to discern what it is that God is calling him to be or do. Through discernment with his director, he has come to see and understand that his gifts lie in teaching children. He has experienced no particular sensory sign, but he has nurtured his natural gifts and feels inclined toward teaching. This choice has been affirmed and supported by others. Thomas believes that this is what call means—desire to do something, attraction toward that particular vocation, gifts and abilities to carry out work in that area, affirmation and support of his vocation, and making sure that what he has chosen to do is in keeping with his Christian upbringing and values. Thomas is pursuing his call by enrolling in a university and by majoring in early childhood education with teaching accreditation.

Not all of us are called to professional, full-time, or or-dained ministry. Thomas isn't, yet he is *called by God* to recognize his gifts and to use them for the good of the community—to implement his piece of God's vision by serving God and his brothers and sisters—as a teacher.

God is the one who calls us; God is the caller, who chooses to be in loving relationship with humanity.

God is calling each one of us, and the authority of call comes from this source—God (Farnham et al. 12). We do not need to ask God to call us; we need only to be open to hear the call that is there from God. We can *ask* to be called, but we cannot *make* it happen (Finley 29). Our abil-ity to wait indicates our readiness to receive. By develop-ing what I call "habits of attentiveness to God's presence in our lives," we can enhance our readiness to receive God's call. To do this, it is helpful to be in relationship with God. I have developed six possible ways we can de-velop this "attentiveness" so that we can be more aware of and receptive to God's presence and call in our lives.

We can develop habits of attentiveness to God's pres-ence by:

1. becoming more open to God in our lives—As much
   as we might say we want to be open to God, we
   sabotage our own efforts by trying to separate
   ourselves from the world and from our everyday
   lives. Openness to God does not involve moving
   away from the world or from others, for we

experience God both in everyday experiences and through other people. Openness to God involves moving more deeply within ourselves while still in the world. It is an attitude that is both innate and intuitive, and it is also an attitude that can be learned. To open ourselves to God, within ourselves and through others, takes risk and trust and faith because we do not know what the specific outcomes of our encounters will be. Most of all, openness involves desire—desire to be in relationship with God.

We can develop habits of attentiveness to God's presence by:

2. developing an awareness of God in our lives—God is already present in us and in our lives, even though we are not always aware of God's presence. When I teach my students counseling skills, we spend time on nonverbal communication. Some say that up to 80 percent of our communication with each other is nonverbal, yet we seem to be unaware of this. It is the same in our communication with God. God is always interacting with us—often nonverbally—yet we are often unaware of it. If we believe that God is mostly or only present at church, or that only those who are holy or who are called to ordained or professional ministry experience God's call, then we will miss God being present elsewhere. We will miss God's call in our lives in our everyday events and in our everyday relationships with others. Developing an awareness of God's call in our lives will involve

21

reexamining our faith. It will involve reexamining who God is to us.

An example of this occurred one night at the dining table when my family began talking about God. My daughter, Deepa, who was then twelve, quite eloquently explained her image of God—that God is neither male nor female and both male and female. There is hope for the next generation, I thought to myself. My son, Micah, who was then eight, put in his vote for a God who is "definitely male." He had once before told me God was male because God spoke to him in a deep voice. Seeing my disappointment with his response, he continued on. God was still male for Micah, but he did think it was possible that God has an assistant and that the assistant is a female. After all, he reasoned, when God comes down to earth from heaven, someone has to be left in charge in heaven, and this could be a female, assistant God. Although this may sound a lot like Santa and Mrs. Claus, I was impressed by how much God was a part of my son's life: he had definite images, and God spoke to him on a regular basis. My son was also open to expanding, changing, or at least re-examining his image of God when he discovered that his image was not "big" enough to cover what happened (in his mind) when God left heaven.

We can develop habits of attentiveness to God's presence by:

3. being attentive to God—When we attend to other people we are present to them physically,

emotionally, socially, and spiritually. We focus our attention on them and listen to what they are saying to us and how they present themselves to us. We do this in the privacy of counseling offices and confessionals, but we also do this in the midst of crowded rooms and on buses and in grocery stores. We do not leave the world to do this. We center ourselves within the world and focus our attention and energy on the other person. I would suggest that the same is necessary for God. As God "speaks" to us, whether in private prayer or through another person, we need to be present to God, to pay attention to what God is saying and doing. In the field of counseling, Gerard Egan uses the acronym SOLER, which suggests a certain posture, a stance that is helpful for listening (91-93):

S—sit squarely;

O—open posture;

L—lean slightly forward;

E—make eye contact;

R—relax!

We need a similar posture to listen to God.

We can develop habits of attentiveness to God's presence by:

4. listening with ears and hearts in the context of our lives—It is not such an easy thing—to listen to another. It takes time, energy, presence, and

patience. It takes a real desire to hear. When the other is God, it takes a belief that God is speaking to us. It takes effort on our part to respond to what the other person or God is saying to us. It takes an awareness that we listen with filters and biases that lead us to certain interpretations and conclusions even before the other person or God has finished speaking. We need to be better able to listen to God in our lives. We need to read God's signs of activity within and among us prayerfully and in the context of our lives. This context includes the communities to which we belong, including our community of worship.

We can develop habits of attentiveness to God's presence by:

5. learning the skills of dealing with adversity and obstacles—We do this by developing the gifts of perseverance and patience. We do this by overcoming our own internal and external resistances to changing our perspectives and our behaviors. In relation, for instance, to prayer, there are a number of common resistances or obstacles, such as fear, boredom, failure to see results, lack of familiarity, lack of connection with daily activity and challenges, and a desire to be in control.[3] Any one of these can be used as an excuse not to live a more prayerful life or as an excuse to not understand or respond to God's call in our lives. We need to be able to name, address, and own our own particular resistances and to work at reframing our own

particular style of prayer. This may mean letting go of the idea that one way of praying is the right way.

We can develop habits of attentiveness to God's presence by:

6. being intentional and acknowledging our call—Restlessness, discomfort, dissatisfaction, and expectancy are signs that God is calling us, as are delight, relief, pleasure, and fulfillment. But we often do not recognize or identify these feelings as signs of God's call. We need to recognize and acknowledge that God's call is a part of all our lives. The process of discernment (detailed in chapter two) will be possible only when we name God and God's call as part of the process. In naming God's call we need to *listen well*, which requires that we be *accurate* in how we listen to God and others. We do this by truly listening to what God is saying, not hearing what we *want* God to say. We then verify our understanding by bringing that understanding to prayer, to a spiritual guide, and to community, particularly a worshiping community of faith.

By developing these habits of attentiveness, we are more likely to recognize God's call. Myers lists three ways to recognize God's call when it is a call to ministry (236-7):

1. The call will be experienced as an "irresistible urge."

2. There will be a recognition among the community of believers.

3. The callee will be committed to prepare for ministry.

Whereas these are helpful signs to look for to recognize a call, there may be unexpected roadblocks that distort the discerner's ability to experience the call and have the call sanctioned. I will address these roadblocks in chapter five.

Those who experience God's call must respond. For those who experience God's call, a repositioning occurs—in order to hear God better or to avoid what God is saying.

It is impossible not to respond to God's call in our lives. Whether the call is a gentle nudge or an incessant pulling, we will eventually respond to God's call. William Myers describes six recurrent stages he found to be dominant in the call stories he studied (8):

1. early religious exposure

2. call experience

3. struggle

4. search

5. support

6. surrender

After we have experienced a call—whether internally, externally, or both—most of us then *struggle* with the call (unlike Linda). According to Myers, "Resisting the call is one of the most prevalent aspects of the struggle" (37). I would call this a repositioning; we have experienced God's call, but we try to move away from it. This desire to reposition ourselves away from the call would be most common for those of us for whom the call evokes such feelings as confusion, anger, shock, or fear. Myers groups those who resist the call into six categories (43-5):

1. the sons and daughters of ministers who try their best *not* to be like Mom or Dad

2. women because of the lack of women as models, or because of the belief that women can't be called, as in the Roman Catholic church and in certain African-American churches

3. youth because they are too young to do what God is asking of them

4. those who are afraid of being inadequate

5. those with other desires for life

6. those with no model of ministry

Resisters reposition themselves by ignoring, denying, delaying, and even defying God's call, hoping it will go away. Resisters "appease" God by going into an "alternate ministry" of service such as medicine or law or by doing something unworthy to prove God is wrong in calling them to ministry (44).

I was a resister, falling under the categories of 2, 3, and 6. I was a young woman with no role model and part of a church that taught I could not be called to the priesthood. I also tried to go into an "alternate ministry" of pastoral counseling.

We who *accept* God's call also reposition ourselves in relation to God. Having heard God's call in our lives, and probably responding to it with feelings corresponding more to delight, acceptance, and happiness, "accepters" (my term) reposition ourselves to remain open to God's guidance so that we may continue to experience God's call in our lives. We move *toward* God and toward fulfilling our call. Linda and Thomas are examples of accepters.

Three additional points should be noted here:

1. Most resisters eventually become accepters and move toward God. We experience the joy that acceptance and closeness to God brings.

2. Many of us experience a range of feelings in relation to our call. Even we who experience more immediate joy and acceptance can also experience the pain and sorrow that the losses involved in responding to call brings.

3. Some of us who desire to accept and live out our call are caught *in between*[4] resistance and acceptance. Or perhaps we are caught in acceptance and unable to move to fulfillment because of circumstances beyond our immediate control.

Circumstances inform our call; circumstances may make our call easier or harder to hear and easier or harder to accept and fulfill; tied to this is the understanding that call is both individual and communal.

For Thomas, the call was an internal one which he experienced in his relationship with God. This call was nurtured and affirmed and supported by his spiritual guide and by his family and friends. Neither society nor the church had any reservations about his call, and he was encouraged to pursue it with all his heart. Thus, positive, nurturing circumstances shaped Thomas' call and blessed him on his journey.[5]

For others, like myself, circumstances may have a negative effect on shaping a call. For instance, when I first experienced my call as a call to the ordained priesthood, I was unable to accept that possibility because I was a female Roman Catholic. The church, the "circumstances" under which I was living, contributed to my struggle with hearing my call. If the Roman Catholic Church had been ordaining women at the time I first heard my call, I would have understood my call much earlier than I did.

Circumstances, then, can shape how we as individuals experience God's call. Much that has been written on call emphasizes the individual experience of God's call, highlighting the primacy of an individual's relationship with God. However, as we have seen, what the community of faith believes has a profound effect on how we experience God's call. Many of us would agree that the community of faith plays an important role in validating an individual's call. We have not, however, fully realized how the community might *prevent* a person from even hearing a call in the first place. My community of faith, the Roman Catholic Church, denied that I even had a call. The Sacred Congregation for the Doctrine of the Faith wrote in their 1976 document, "Declaration on the Question of the Admission of Women to the Ministerial Priesthood":

> It is sometimes said and written in books and periodicals that some women feel that they have a voca-

tion to the priesthood. Such an attraction, however noble and understandable, still does not suffice for a genuine vocation. In fact a vocation cannot be reduced to a mere personal attraction which can remain purely subjective. Since the priesthood is a particular ministry of which the Church has received the charge and the control, authentication by the Church is indispensable here and is a constitutive part of the vocation....

Women who express a desire for the ministerial priesthood are doubtless motivated by the desire to serve Christ and the Church.... But it must not be forgotten that the priesthood does not form part of the rights of the individual, but stems from the economy of the mystery of Christ and the Church. The priestly office cannot become the goal of social advancement... (17).

Whereas I agree that a community can deny me formal recognition and authentication of my call, I cannot accept the negation of my experiencing the call itself.[6]

The words from the Sacred Congregation for the Doctrine of the Faith were written when I was in seminary studying for my Master of Divinity degree and preparing for ministry. Even as I re-read these words twenty years later, I feel a great sadness. As a counselor I have come to understand that one of the greatest mistakes I can make in counseling is to tell a person how she feels or to tell her that what she is experiencing or feeling is wrong. And yet that is what the Congregation for the Doctrine of Faith told me twenty years ago and what the official, institutional church continues to tell me. This has led me to redefine what church means to me and who my community is. I have found support and affirmation of my call within the Roman Catholic Church, by individuals and by groups, but I have not found acceptance or affirmation by the hierarchy of the church.

Myers refers to a similar phenomenon of denial and lack of affirmation that has occurred in the African-American churches. The women whom he interviewed went to others seeking clarity and authentication of their call, but some were told by their pastor that the pastor could not sanction their call because of their gender. This was not true with the men whom he interviewed; whereas men faced resistance from others because of "economics, expectations, age or some other factor, [it was] never gender" (231). These women were prevented from bringing their call to their community—just like Roman Catholic women—by men in authority positions.

This search for *validation* that I have a call and *sanction* that it is a call from God and it is seen and blessed by others can be pivotal in the discernment process because

> the solitary experience with God is not enough to validate the call. Those called seem to need human validation. Even if they don't get it and instead receive validation from some event that clinches the call experience for them, they still seek human validation from people in the community of faith, especially those who have had this kind of experience and subsequently were validated themselves (53).

Responding to call means realizing that this process involves loss and that, in order to move through the discernment process, we must also concurrently move through the grieving process.

The above statement forms both the foundation for this book and the link that holds it together. Each subsequent chapter will address some aspect of this statement.

Chapter Two

Discern the Call

To speak of discernment[1] presupposes an understanding of or experience of call. The two are so intimately related that it is hard to speak of one without the other, and thus the division of this book into separate chapters on call and discernment is rather artificial. We *continue* to discern after hearing or receiving a call, and call is *part* of discerning. Discernment is part of the broader context of spirituality, prayer, and faith. As such, it is "a loving vigilance toward God, others and the world that seeks to do the truth in love" (Mueller 129).

To "enter into" a process of discernment implies that we have sensed a call, even if we have not named it as such. To "enter into" discernment means we shift our spiritual posture to become more open and ready. We desire to be in close relationship with God and to hear more of what God is saying to us. We become more curious and courageous; we become more willing to be in contact and communication with God. We turn our attention to the questions: What is my experience of God? Where is God leading me? What are my gifts? (Anderson, "What Consoles?" 234).

To speak of discernment is to speak of spirituality and of the Spirit, which acts within us, helping us to name our awareness of this activity (Larkin 9). It is to speak of a "habit of faith" that disposes us to hear the word of God and respond (Johnson 110). We have experienced God's call in our lives, the Spirit's stirrings—as vague or as specific as that may be. We have opened ourselves up to this call or this activity and have acknowledged our desire to better understand what that call means and what we need to do about it. We have looked at what our gifts are and what they mean in relation to our sense of call. We have identified the Caller as God (Who?); we seek clarification on the message (What?) and the method (How?); we wonder about the reasons (Why me?). We may never know the reasons but we can learn to accept the unknown (Why?).

We find ourselves in a time of transition or crisis. We are clear that God is calling us, that the Spirit is alive within us, and we find we can no longer remain still or quiet. Discernment involves movement: the movement of the Spirit within us, movement in our relationship with God, and the movement with which we respond to God's call.

If we have experienced a dramatic or cataclysmic call, we may already be clear about *what* God is asking of us, and our attention will be on the *how* to fulfill our call. But for some, the call is more general, and the first step of the discernment process will be to clarify the call. To do this, we must clearly state what we are trying to discern and be willing to devote time and energy to discernment (Mueller 9).

Discernment[2] is a process of listening to God's call and prayerfully reflecting on that call. It involves clarifying our understanding of our call by gathering information and again prayerfully reflecting on our understanding of our call. It involves bringing our understanding to others and seeking advice and validation. Finally, discernment involves responding to what we have heard, felt, and understood by deciding and acting wisely.

Listen and prayerfully reflect on our call

In order to listen and prayerfully reflect on our call, we must create an internal "climate" for discernment (Green 55). We must prepare ourselves to be open and attentive, to receive and listen. Green (58-61) cites three preconditions of discernment:

1. a desire to do God's will

2. openness to God

3. knowledge of God

As we prayerfully reflect on our experience of call we examine our relationship with God. Do we desire to be in a closer relationship with God? Are we open to what God wants of us? Do we know this God with whom we are relating? Are we comfortable in how we are communicating?

Prayerful reflection does not mean that we have to separate ourselves from the world in order to pray, although this may be *part* of prayerful reflection. This is not the time to worry how we are going to go through this whole process in its entirety. It is a time of preparation, of grounding, and of formation. It is a time of fueling our desire to be in relationship with God, to be in a process of discernment and movement.

Patricia was clear on her call to ministry, but she was reluctant to act on it. Before she chose to involve herself in a process of discernment she had to spend time on her relationship with God and her attitude toward God and life. She had to name her emotions—particularly her uncertainties and fears. Mostly she had to get in the habit of including God in her daily life, of bringing her concerns to God on a daily basis. She did this by letting go of her past relationship with God, much of which she saw as a failure. She was then free to open herself up to what was happening *now*.[3] She invited God into her everyday living and looked for God in everything she did.

Clarify our understanding of call by gathering information

For Patricia, the clarity was there, and she spent her time on other steps of the process. But for Anne, the call was much more vague; others recognized it, but she did not. She felt restless, confused, and uncertain. After making prayer a part of her discernment process and opening herself up to continue the process, she focused on clarifying *what* her call was.

Most of us do not receive blueprints for our call, even if we are clear on what our call is. Or, as Larkin says, the Spirit does not give us specific answers. We gain clarity by the feelings of reassurance, peace, joy, and love that we experience as we try to interpret what our call is (39). We feel empowered and strengthened as we move *toward* understanding. We seek out a pastor, a spiritual director, a friend or relative to help us make sense of what we are feeling.

We listen to our deepest self and trust our insights that come from our feelings (Fischer 114-117). There is a connection between our heartfelt desires and what God's will is for us.

Thomas Hart proposes some guidelines for discernment, which I have put in the format of a simple exercise (77):

Fill in the blanks:

I want _____ .

I would like _____ .

I feel like _____ .

I should _____ .

I respond to these statements in the following way:

I want *to be a priest* (wholeheartedly).

I would like *to be finished with this book* (a temporary wish).

I feel like *taking a long vacation* (but I probably won't).

I should *read more than I do* (what I believe others expect of me).

We tap into our resources, our faith tradition, and our support systems. We are comforted to discover that "God not only calls but empowers—although the power may come only as we respond" (Farnham et al. 15). As scary as it feels to enter into this process of discernment, the alternative is to remain stuck in our relationship with God, stuck in our uncertainty and discomfort, stagnant and un-fulfilled—not a very appealing prospect. Because "if we don't respond to God's call, we may cut ourselves off from the Lord's strength and become increasingly blind and deaf to God's promptings" (Farnham et al. 15).

Naming our call is pivotal here. In naming our call, we gain power and strength to continue. For some of us the call quickly becomes clear, and we move on. For others lack of clarity remains our greatest roadblock in the dis-cernment process. Lack of clarity may be due to circum-stances surrounding our call where clarity is circumvented by dissonance and apparent contradiction. "You are called to be an ordained priest, Roslyn." The call was clear. Yet I could not name the call so clearly since it seemed impossible.

For Thomas clarity came quickly, and he moved on to other parts of the process. For Patricia clarity came quickly, but she resisted moving on. For Anne clarity was much more gradual and continues to evolve as she continues to discern.

Prayerfully reflect on our understanding of our call by bringing our own experience of call to another

In this part of the discernment process, we need to hear ourselves tell another of our call. We need to give voice to our call and tell our story of call to another human being. We need to see how they respond to what we have said. *Who* we choose to tell our story to is determined by a number of factors: whom do we trust? Who will under-stand? What tradition do we come from? Myers writes that in the African-American church tradition it is likely, even expected, that parishioners will go to their pastor with their call story, though they may initially entrust this information with a beloved relative (59-60). Who we tell is also reflective of our personalities and our personal needs. Do we want to be affirmed or told that we are mistaken? Do we want someone who will listen without comment or judgment, or do we want someone who will ask us questions and give us advice?

I chose to share my call story with no one until I reached college, when my call had become clearer. Then I chose to confide in my mentor—a Roman Catholic lay man who I knew supported an expanded role for women in the church. He was for me a safe, sensitive, and affirming person.

He heard my call and affirmed it, but the fulfillment of my call was blocked by the institutional church. Some of us are rejected when we tell our call story to another. This was the case with Ellen who chose to tell her pastor of her call to the priesthood. He told her, "You are a woman; you cannot be called by God to ordained ministry." When this occurs it is necessary to remind ourselves that discernment is just and oppression is not the fruit of the Holy Spirit (Mueller 9).

A second part of this step is to share our call with a broader, larger community, such as an ordination committee, a discernment group, a small Christian community, or our congregation. For some this may come much later in the process.

Respond to the clarified and initially affirmed call

As Farnham et al. point out, call requires response and obedience (14). When we speak to someone we expect a response—verbal or nonverbal. We expect a person to be present to us physically and emotionally, and perhaps even spiritually. This presence is shown nonverbally through eye contact, head nodding, and facial expressions such as raised eyebrows, smiles, frowns, and furrowed brows. We also expect verbal communication.

This is also what God desires of us—that we be present and attentive to what God is saying. If we accept that God is the initiator, the one who calls (see chapter one), then it is up to us to respond to that call by being present to God—physically, emotionally, and spiritually. We do this by being nonjudgmental, by being open to what we do not want to hear, and by relinquishing control of the conversation. We accept that we are the listeners and God is in charge of the conversation. We assume an open and receptive posture, a posture of being present to God. We become more aware of God's presence already within us.

We also need to respond verbally to God's call. We need to talk to God, much as we respond to any person who converses with us. We do this by using the skills of clarifying, empathy, self-disclosure, and advanced empathy (Egan 106-121, 140-41, 180-86).

Clarifying what we have heard

We clarify the call in a number of ways: we ask questions, we repeat what we have heard, we ask the other person (in this case God), if we have heard correctly, and even ask to have the call repeated—perhaps in a different way so that we can better understand what we have heard. How much we need to use this skill will depend on how clearly we have heard our call. We also gain clarity by talking with others about our call.

Using empathy to see if we have heard correctly what was "said"

Empathy is defined as the ability to walk in another's shoes, to understand the world from the other's perspective. The skill of empathy involves trying to understand what God (the other) means. We convey our understanding nonverbally (nodding our head), but also verbally (Egan 110-116) by giving voice to our understanding— "Let me see if I have this right; you are asking me to serve you through teaching"—and seeing how God and others respond to our understanding.

Self-disclosing ourselves and our lives to God

If we are resisting the call our self-disclosure may consist of sharing with God all the reasons we cannot possibly do what God is asking of us. If we are clear on the call, and accept it, we may also use the skill of self-disclosure by continuing to bring to God all the events, experiences, and feelings of our lives and sharing these with God in conversation and prayer.

Identifying our hunches and checking them out with advanced empathy

The final skill that may be helpful is *advanced empathy*, especially if we are having difficulty in responding because of a lack of clarity. Advanced empathy is a skill that draws upon our intuition and helps us to read between the lines. We have a sense, a feeling, or a *hunch* about what is being said, what is going on within us, but we are not sure. And so we express our hunch and check it out with God and with others. We do not use this skill early on in discernment or early on in our relationship with God or with others; we have to "know" God well enough to form a hunch. We have to know God or others well enough to check out our hunch.

This conversation with God—checking out our understanding of God's call—can take many forms, the primary form being prayer. The way we pray will depend on our personality types.[4] I personally am more drawn to what has traditionally been called kataphatic prayer—prayer that pays attention to images, thoughts, sensations, and emotions—to become aware of God's presence, rather than apophatic prayer, which is imageless prayer that emphasizes the unknowable mystery of God. Whichever type of prayer we are drawn to, we will need some sort of companion or guide to help us in our prayer. In the Roman Catholic tradition this person has been known as a spiritual director or a spiritual guide.

My own struggle was that I believed that a more contemplative and apophatic style of prayer was the *preferred* way to talk with God. I struggled to silence my naturally extroverted, people-oriented, and image-filled self. It was only in reframing and owning my own concept of spirituality that I was able to make progress in my prayer life and thus in my discernment process. Although I had chosen what might be defined as the "active life," I also believed I *should* be drawn to a more contemplative life—as a Christian and certainly as a Christian minister. I lived out internally what I believe has existed externally for centuries: the battle between the active and the contemplative life, which for me also involved a battle between extroversion and introversion.[5] In the ancient world, the contemplative life was more highly valued than the active life (desert fathers and mothers, rise of monasticism). With the Age of Exploration and Enlightenment and the Industrial Revolution, the active life has gained in value. In the post-Vatican II church there is a high value placed on active living yet there is still a desire for contemplation. It seems as if we are continuing to set up action and contemplation as contradictory categories that exclude each other. Parker Palmer has helped me to reframe this image to one of contemplation and action, not as contradictory categories, but poles of a paradox (7). "People called to active life need to nurture a spirituality that does not fear the vitalities of action" (7-8). Instead of separating the two, there is the possibility of integrating the two, or of coming to a point of integration—where we live a life of activity *and* contemplation, where the yin and yang of living spiritually are not opposites, not either/or, but both/and (15).

For me, contemplative prayer has involved discovery, awareness, change in perspective, re-creation and self-discovery. It has involved openness and awareness and a willingness to go deeper within my heart while still in the world.

This part of the discernment process involves both contemplation and action. It involves becoming a more spiritual person. Being a more spiritual person presupposes that I have a definition of spirituality out of which I live and out of which I respond.

Spirituality means being directed toward, attuned to, and responsive to the Spirit of God in a particular time and place (Premnath 2). It means to seek God, experience God, and do God's work in the world; it is a balance of action and contemplation. The goal is the recovery of wholeness within ourselves, between us and others, and between us and God (van den Blink 1994).

Spirituality encompasses our relations to all creation and is expressed in everything we do (Carr 49). It is an ever-deepening inwardness and an ever-extending outwardness (Premnath 3). It involves a relationship in which God takes the initiative (McMakin and Nary 24); we need to be attuned so we can discern what God is doing, where God is acting (Premnath 2), what God requires of us. It is a commitment to self, God, and others (Wicks 8) and involves openness, sensitivity, responsiveness, availability (Duraisingh 5), and risk (Doohan 104). Finally, and foundationally, spirituality involves prayer.

How to become more spiritual will differ from person to person. Wicks offers five helpful suggestions to guide the process (39):

1. Letting go,

2. Being in the now,

3. Appreciating the value of experiencing deep gratitude,

4. Knowing the impact of having a greater openness to passion and awe,

5. Seeking and maintaining a simple sense of perspective.

Bringing our understanding of our call to others for advice and validation

This involves recognizing what is of God and what is not, putting aside our own assumptions and trying to be open to new possibilities.

Much of what I have emphasized thus far is the personal, individual relationship that we have with God and our experience of God's call. Some may see this as over-emphasizing the importance of the individual call experience, yet this emphasis is pivotal to the process. It is too often ignored—particularly for women in the church.

One summer I taught a class with four students—a Baptist, a Unitarian-Universalist, an Episcopalian, and a Roman Catholic. The Baptist student was sharing his distress with the students in the class, whom he assumed believed the way that he did. He told the following story:

> I was in (another) class this morning and we were talking about why we came to seminary. I talked about the day I had accepted Jesus Christ into my life as my Lord and Savior. Some people in the class couldn't understand what I was saying. Can you imagine that? What are they doing in seminary?

The Roman Catholic responded:

> Well, we might *mean* the same thing, or have similar
> reasons for being here, but I wouldn't use the same
> language that you do. I don't remember a particular
> day when I accepted Jesus into my life. He's always
> been a part of what it means to be a Christian.

It was that day I realized that my own biases were with
the Baptist student, particularly in relation to call to ministry. Why else am I in ministry if not in response to God's
personal call? I have found that many agree with me, but I
have been surprised to find how vague that call has been
for many. And so, although I still believe that the individual
experience of call is crucial, I have come to realize that not
everyone receives the specific and clear call that I received.

The process of checking out our call with others involves movement and change in the discernment process.
The call is no longer between us and God. Its validity and
viability are being held up for others—to bless or to curse,
to sanction or to dismiss. According to Myers this sanction of
our call is necessary to be able to go on to the final step of discernment—what he calls surrender, involving acknowledgment, announcement, and acceptance of the call (61).

We have clarified and reflected on our call and received
some initial affirmation. We have also experienced signs of
peace, serenity, joy, clarity, and convergence and a persist-
ence in the calling (Farnham et al. 46-47). We now continue in this process bringing our call to community for
new insights, help in listening, information, challenge, encouragement, support, and further instruction. Farnham et
al. suggest one possible place to bring our call would be to

a "discernment group," whose goal would be to help us in our continued discernment. The group helps us to discern whether the call is of God or not and helps us to see and understand more than our limited individual perspective may see (55). One way this is determined by the group is to see whether our call involves service or benefit to others; if this is so, the call is more likely to be of God (13). Farnham et al. suggest a number of questions that the discernment group can ask the discerner such as: Do you have a vision of your ministry? How would you advise someone else with a similar issue? What motivates you? What are your present commitments? Who has influenced you? What does Scripture say to you? (88-89). If a discerner is specifically seeking help with a call to ordained ministry, the group might ask additional questions: Why are you seeking ordination? Are your abilities appropriate to ordained ministry? How do others perceive you? Does your call come from your faith community? Are you able to pursue seminary studies? Are you aware of the demands placed on an ordained minister? (90-91).

The group is helpful to the discerner in a number of ways. It can help the discerner to determine if he or she has a call, what the call is to, what gifts the discerner has for ministry, and what further resources and information the discerner needs.

John Wesley's questions (as quoted in "The Ordained Ministry" para. 403) for those presenting themselves as candidates for ordained ministry are similar to Farnham et al.'s:

> 1. Do they know God as a pardoning God? Have they the love of God abiding in them? Do they

desire nothing but God? Are they holy in all manner of conversation?

2. Have they gifts, as well as evidence of God's grace, for the work? Have they a clear, sound understanding; a right judgment in the things of God; a just conception of salvation by faith? Do they speak justly, readily, clearly?

3. Have they fruit? Have any been truly convinced of sin and converted to God, and are believers edified by their preaching?

   As long as these marks concur in them, we believe they are called of God to preach. These we receive as sufficient proof that they are moved by the Holy Spirit.

Morton Kelsey also believes in the importance of broadening our understanding of discernment by looking at whether what is influencing an individual or group is "angelic" or "demonic" (82). He lists eight criteria for determining whether the influence is of God; I will mention three of these criteria (82-83):

1. Is the action being considered in accord with a tradition or not? If it in no way relates to a tradition, then this is a danger signal that the action is not divine.

2. Will the action result in harmony and love or hate and schism?

3. Will the action "result in the fruits[6] of creativity, growth, development, increased consciousness and keener awareness?"

These are helpful and important guidelines, because our accountability is not only to God, but also to a community of faith (Farnham et al. 71). However, these guidelines may need to be adjusted in the case of Roman Catholic women and in other instances of "complicated discernment" (see chapter five).

Enrique Dussell, writing from a liberationist perspective, also underscores this necessity for a communal context to discernment:

> Those who claim to recognize spirits with the help of their individual conscience alone, on its own, will in the end find only the interests of the ruling class…. The only guarantee that discernment can be truly and historically orthodox…is for it to be linked to the praxis of the liberation of the poor…in which practical judgment has its beginning and its end (58).

Whereas most would agree that discernment involves cooperation with and conversation with legitimate authority (Mueller 9), it is not to be drawn only from the "interests of the ruling class" (Dussell 58), for the Spirit gives preference to the poor, the young and the vulnerable (Mueller 15).

It is helpful for the discerner to have his or her own questions to ask of the group: Is my call of God? Do you see in me the ability and gifts to carry out a call to ministry? Can you help me in clarifying the specific forms my ministry should take? Am I putting up unnecessary roadblocks, or am I missing roadblocks that I need to be aware of? Do you support and affirm me in my call to ministry?

Thus far I have described the process of discernment as having a sense of call and bringing that sense to a community for affirmation. I have also indicated that the community may put up roadblocks to our call that prevent us from pursuing our call. For instance, a community may not even *listen* to our call story. Yet listening to *all* stories does not mean saying *yes* to every story. At the very least we (discerners) need to be allowed to tell our story, and the church needs to be clear on why it is saying no to us (Johnson 11).

There is also the possibility that the community can affirm a call that is not there. Leigh Sutcliffe Ramsey has described a three-fold process that she has developed in response and resistance to her faith community, which tried to convince her she had a call to ordained ministry when she did not feel she did (12).[7] I have found it a helpful corrective to my thinking that the community supports or blocks our *already experienced call* to ministry. Ramsey had not experienced a call to ordained ministry; her community informed her of her call. The first step in Ramsey's process is *disillusionment*—when, through reflection, we attempt to clear away misleading appearances from the vision. She lists as possible misleading appearances the community's or pastor's agenda and the lure of being needed. The second step is *resistance*, which she defines as "standing in opposition to a force, not being overcome by it." In this step we resist the pressure of the community and pay attention to our own experience and feelings. Finally, we *imagine*—"critically reflective discernment free from community illusion and oppression with the added dimension of seeing the possibilities for the future." This step completes disillusionment and resistance and frees us to envision an alternative future. This gives clarity and choice to the discerner.

Deciding and acting wisely

This step brings the discernment process full circle. We enter the discernment process in order to make a decision about call; it is at this step that this decision is made and the process returns to its beginning. In this step we have drawn together the resources of our faith tradition, individual and communal prayer, Scripture, and individual and community response. We have consulted with friends, family, pastor, mentor, spiritual guide, and community. We have heard, clarified, prayed, reflected, responded, decided, and we are now ready to act on what we have gathered and heard. This action will take various forms: acceptance of call and decision to pursue our call; acceptance of a call to ordained ministry; realization that our call is not to ordained ministry but to another vocation; awareness that our call is to ordained ministry in a church that will not ordain us because of our gender; a decision to remain in our church community; a decision to leave our church.

When we are clear about our call and choose to stay within a church that does not affirm that call, particularly because of our gender, the discernment process takes on what I refer to as "complications." Complications may occur because of obstacles that hinder us from gaining clarity about the call itself. Complications may occur in hearing, in understanding, in accepting, or in validating the call. The discernment process can be complicated by circumstances and context. The discernment process can also be complicated because we have failed to recognize that discernment includes a series of losses which we must mourn and move through. God is calling us to be someone *different* than we are. It is in recognizing and naming and grieving the losses we encounter in this differentness that we can better navigate the process of discernment.

Chapter Three

Understand the Call in Relation to Loss and Grief

C hapters one and two look at what it means to be called by God and how we discern and clarify God's call in our life. In describing the process of discernment, I note that *loss* is a part of the steps of discernment and that *grief* is a reaction to the various losses we experience. This chapter looks more specifically at the concepts of loss and grief, developing a framework of understanding loss and grief that will inform us and aid us in our discernment process and in guiding others in their discernment process.

Chapters three and four suggest that the discernment process and the grieving process overlap and need to be named, recognized, and addressed as such. Linking the discernment process with the grieving process allows the discerner to realize further possibilities for healing and growth and for working through the discernment process.

What is grief?

To begin with, we need to note that the model of grief that I am describing and working out of is grief as reaction to loss (Parkes). There are at least two other models of grief: grief as separation anxiety (Sullivan and Switzer) and grief as a function of attachment instincts (Freud, Bowlby, Parkes, and William Rogers) (Sullender 243-251).

Grief is a normal, natural, emotional response to a *perceived, significant loss*; it is a response that occurs over and over again. It is unique and individual, and it is also universal and unavoidable. It is "a wound that needs attention in order to heal" (Tatelbaum 9). *Everyone* experiences grief because all significant losses give rise to grief. As humans we all experience significant losses.

The experience of *loss* encompasses and includes grief and the grieving process; it occurs over time and is not tied to only a discrete event. Mitchell and Anderson have identified six major types of loss (35-46):

1. material loss—the loss of a physical object that is valuable or important to us; this loss is first experienced when we are children; includes broken toys, discarded teddy bears, and pets.

2. relationship loss—the loss of opportunity to share experiences with and be in the emotional or physical presence of another; includes moving, divorce, change in job, and death.

3. intrapsychic loss—the loss of an image of ourself, of plans for the future or the loss of dreams; an inward experience occurring for the first time in

adolescence; often unknown to others because we have kept our plans and dreams a secret; loss of faith.

4. functional loss—the loss of muscular or neurological functions of the body; includes actual loss of memory, sight, or hearing which occurs as part of the aging process.

5. role loss—the loss of a specific role; includes retirement, promotion, entering school in midlife, graduation, and marriage.

6. systemic loss—a loss experienced by a system, i.e., a family or an entire community; loss of someone with a pivotal role or place in the system. For example, the young adult's departure from his or her family of origin; a pastor's departure from a parish.

By understanding the concept of loss in this broad way, we can see that we all experience numerous losses in our lifetime. We can also begin to appreciate that some losses will be more difficult than others because of the *type* of the loss, the *timing* of the loss, the *type of relationship* with the person or the object lost, or the *manner and circumstances* of the loss. (See chapter five for more on difficult loss and difficult grieving.)

Grieving is also a process that occurs over time; it involves a number of stages, phases, dimensions, or clusters of experiences and feelings. We can sometimes choose *not* to grieve, and we can certainly be *told* not to grieve.

The distinction that I wish to emphasize here is between *grief* and *grieving*: we all experience grief, but we do not all *grieve*.[1]

When we use the word *grief*, we often mean *grieving*, for grief is really our *initial* reaction to loss, and *grieving* is the *continuation* of that reaction. Therefore, I will often use the word grieving, where the reader might be more accustomed to seeing the word grief.

Although stage theory has been criticized in recent years,[2] I still find it helpful to have a flexible understanding of the different "stages," or what I would prefer to call "dimensions" of grieving. This understanding is helpful as long as we are able to keep in mind that grief is not systematic or linear; it does not go neatly from stage to stage, and the dimensions may overlap.

Many authors have written of these stages of grieving. To simplify our understanding, I have summarized the work of a number of authors.[3]

Stages or dimensions of grieving

Alarm, shock, disbelief, retreating, avoidance, panic, physical symptoms of distress

When we experience a significant loss—the death of a child, divorce, the loss of a job, retirement—our first reactions are usually shock and disbelief: "This is not happening to me"; "This can't be so"; "I don't believe it"; "I can't deal with this." Most significant losses evoke this initial feeling response as the shock of the significance of the loss overwhelms us and the body, mind, and spirit struggle to cope with the loss. These feeling responses are often accompanied with physical symptoms such as loss of weight, inability to sleep, decreased sexual interest, crying, fatigue, lack of strength, shortness of breath, or heart palpitations.[4]

These initial responses usually only last a few weeks unless prolonged by artificial means (i.e., alcohol, tranquilizers) or unless prolonged by the severity and the violence of the loss (i.e., murder, multiple deaths, suicide).

Yearning and searching

This dimension of grief may be described as an intense desire for what or who was lost. We display a "strong urge to find, recover, and reunite with the lost person" (Rando, *Grief, Dying, and Death* 25) or object. Our urge becomes a *preoccupation* and we experience an intense pining. We are restless and angry, and we may experience the illusion of actually seeing the deceased or lost person. We feel drawn toward places or objects associated with the deceased or lost person. This phase involves coming home from work and hearing our child's voice, or smelling our husband's cologne, and searching the house for them, even though we "know" they are no longer there.

Acute mourning: disorganization, depression, and despair evoking emotions of guilt, loneliness, relief, anger and continuing physical symptoms; preoccupation with the past; developing awareness, confrontation and resistance

At this stage we give up our searching and yearning. These are the days of not wanting to get out of bed, feeling like we are going crazy, that life is not worth living. This stage feels like it goes on forever, and we are tempted to or may even try to go back to the phase of being numb. We feel overwhelmed by the intensity and duration of the variety of feelings. And just when we believe that we are getting through some of the worst of the pain, a tidal wave of emotion can suddenly overwhelm us and leave us adrift.[5]

Most of the people I counsel either get stuck in this stage or find that they have skipped this stage and need to go back and regrieve a loss and go through this difficult part of the grieving process. This is the most uncomfortable stage—both for ourselves and for those with whom we live and work. We *want* to feel better and others want us to feel better. We are encouraged to get through this stage as quickly as possible.

Socially, we find ourselves restless; we cannot sit still; we are unable to initiate or maintain long periods of activity; we withdraw from social activity (Lindemann).

In our awareness of our loss and our grief, we may also actively *confront* and *resist* the myriad of feelings, the physical symptoms, and the spiritual malaise we experience. This requires of us an energy we do not possess and demands of us that we plod our way through a morass when we would rather run around or jump over it. However, if we do not go through this morass, we will carry around within us all those feelings we are trying so hard to avoid and get over.

A working through or resolving of the loss, a reorganization, reestablishment, or reintegration, a letting go of what was, and the renewed hope for new life

If we have plodded through the middle phases of grief, we will eventually come to a point of being able to "go on" without the lost object or person. This does not mean that we have "gotten over" or even completely "through" the loss. Some major losses will take our lifetime to grieve (Rando, *Treatment of Complicated Mourning* 60-63). But it does mean that we have sufficiently let go of the relationship to be able to form new relationships, to feel hopeful again about life, and to re-enter the social world.

Another way of stating this is to say that we have completed the "tasks" of grieving (Sunderland 37-56), that we have:

1. accepted the reality of the loss

2. accepted that grieving is painful and worked through our painful feelings

3. struggled back from depression and despair

4. decided to take up life again

*****

Thus far I have described the "normal" or "ordinary" grieving process in very general terms. The question remains, however, how do loss, grief, and grieving relate to call and to the discernment process? In order to understand this connection, let us return to two of the people mentioned in chapters one and two: Thomas and Patricia.

Thomas is a 21-year-old single Caucasian male who has been struggling with what God's call is in his life. Through discernment with a spiritual guide, he has come to see that God's call for him is to be a teacher. Thomas can believe and accept that call, and his family and friends support him in his call. There is no apparent conflict or loss. Thomas likes teaching and has the support and resources to pursue this vocation. Yet Thomas has had to experience change and loss to get to where he is. His relationship with God has changed in his discernment process. God is no longer distant and only to be worshipped on Sunday, but ever-present and to be related to on a daily basis. At first glance, most of us would see this as a *gain*; however, for Thomas, this is also loss. Thomas has lost the distant, safe, and not-too-interfering God and replaced that God with one who is always with him. In many ways, the God that Thomas knew before was an easier God to live with, and certainly Thomas' relationship with that God did not require so much work. Thomas is also experiencing other losses as he pursues his education to become a teacher. He finds that the best program for him is in another town and decides to move closer to campus. He leaves behind his parents, close friends, a church community, his family home, and a part-time job.

Patricia is forty-five years old, African-American, Baptist, and a single parent of two children. She felt a call to ordained ministry many years ago, but put that call aside, reluctant to believe what God was calling her to do. Even after accepting her call, she was reluctant to make the changes that following that call would involve. Preparing for ordained ministry would mean leaving a successful job, moving away from family and friends, moving out of, and perhaps even selling her home, and leaving her church community. It would also mean rethinking her dreams for the future as a vice president of the company. She hardly wanted to think of the changes it would mean for her children.

After many years of denying her call, Patricia confided her struggles to her pastor. Her pastor told her that he had known for many years that Patricia was called to ministry and wondered when she would finally do something about it. These words were the encouragement and affirmation that Patricia needed. She resigned from her job and applied to study at a seminary. At first she felt relieved and even peaceful that she was responding to God's call. Soon after arriving at seminary, however, she found herself confused, indecisive, angry, and listless. She began to wonder if she had made the wrong decision or if she had understood the call correctly. She wondered if she should leave.

In their discernment processes we can identify a number of losses Thomas and Patricia experienced. Chapter four will continue this process of naming specific losses and will walk the reader through this recognition and naming. For now it is sufficient that we recognize that losses are part of discernment. Once we recognize this, we will also be able to see that some of these losses are significant enough to evoke from us grief responses, which in turn set into motion a grieving process. This actually occurs whether or not we recognize what is happening but is made easier and less complicated when we are able to name and grieve our losses.

There are three final points to consider in relation to grieving and its effect on the discernment process.

1. Grief, and the process of grieving, is pervasive and can feel like an unwanted, "constant companion" (Sunderland 59). If we do not name our constant companion as grief, we will become confused and anxious, and the process of discernment will be harder and longer than it may need to be. We saw that Patricia was ready to leave seminary. It was in recognizing and then grieving her losses that she made sense of her uneasiness and despair. She could have (mis)read her feelings to be a sign from God that she had misunderstood what God was asking of her. Instead, by grieving her losses, she was able to move on in her discernment, to stay in seminary, and to continue to respond to God's call in her life.

2. **Loss changes us and changes our relationship with God.** Because loss and grieving are processes that occur over time and continue to impact and influence us, they will also change how we see life, what we expect, and who we are. The young girl of eight who was called by God to ministry is not the same adult woman of forty-three who is writing this book. I am older and I hope wiser, but I am also *changed* because of the many losses I have experienced and grieved in my discernment process. Loss has caused me to be more cautious, yet more sensitive, more doubtful, yet more faithful. For example, because I cannot fulfill my call to become a priest within the Roman Catholic Church, I have become more sensitive to others who also face roadblocks in their discernment process: women in other denominations whose church will not ordain them (Missouri Synod Lutheran, Southern Baptist), and non-celibate gays and lesbians in almost every denomination. I am no longer certain that I will be ordained in my lifetime, yet I have become an ever-more-faithful witness to God's presence and the Spirit's movement in my life through my teaching, counseling, and writing.

In recognizing and responding to my call I have also had to realize that my relationship with God has changed, and I have *lost* the relationship I used to have with God. This is good news, for I have lost a distant and apathetic relationship with God and replaced that relationship with an intimate and caring one. However, as good as that may sound, it was actually easier to have a relationship with a God who only spoke to me occasionally and did not seem to ask much of me. The closer I am to God, the more space God takes up in my life, and I sometimes find I miss the days when I could relegate God to a small corner of my life.

Likewise, the more we are aware of loss and grief, the more we realize we have many losses in our life and the more space these losses seem to take up. We now realize that we grieve our graduation and our wedding, what seem to be gains and events to be celebrated. In graduation we grieve our loss of security, the safety of being a student, and our seminary or college community even though we have gained a job; in marriage we grieve the loss of our single life, and our independence even though we have gained a life partner. That this gain *and loss* occurs needs to be recognized, lest we risk holding on to unresolved losses, and thus unnecessary difficulties and complications in the discernment process. Thus, by recognizing these losses, and then grieving them and letting them go, they actually take up less space and create less chaos in our lives.

3. A spiritual goal of grieving *and* discernment is to rediscover God as one who discerns and suffers with us. Our goal is to shift from asking, "Why did God do this to me?" and "Why did God call me?" to "*Who* is this God who suffers with me?" "Who is this God who calls me?" (grieving questions: Mitchell and Anderson 171; call questions, Karaban).

The most often asked question early on in grieving *and* early on in discernment is "why?" Why me? Why now? Why so much pain? These are questions that are asked out of our pain and out of our faith. They are questions we ask as grievers and discerners and questions we are asked as pastoral ministers and spiritual guides.

The most poignant story that I have ever heard regarding the question "Where is God in my suffering?" comes from Elie Wiesel's book, *Night* (75-76). He writes of an incident in a concentration camp in which three men, one of whom was a young boy, were being hanged while the entire camp watched. Because of the boy's light weight, he was taking a long time to die. Wiesel writes that someone near him cried out, "*Where* is God?" Wiesel's response was that God was on the gallows *with* the boy. For Wiesel, it was God's presence that made the incident tolerable (Karaban, *Isaiah* 30).

When I can understand God to be a God who is with me—especially in my most acute pain—I will be more able to converse with this God, and will be more open and able to respond to what this God is asking of me. If I believe that God does not abandon me in my grief, or my loneliness, or my fear, or my uncertainty, I will be more willing to be in relationship with, respond to, and serve this God. I will become less concerned with why God is calling me and why there is pain in my life and more concerned about who this God is. I will want to know all that I can about this God and will search out all the information I can about God. Chapters four and five will continue to address the link between loss, grief, and discernment. Chapter six will address other theological concerns of grieving and discernment by making specific suggestions on how we can respond to those who ask "why?" and those who struggle with complicated discernment.

Part II

How Do We Respond to God's Call?

Chapter Four

Name and Grieve the Losses

In chapter three the emphasis was on recognizing that we experience many losses in our life for which we need to grieve. I defined the grieving process and referred to different types of losses. This chapter continues the emphasis on the importance of recognizing the pervasiveness of loss in our lives and naming it as such, particularly in the discernment process. In naming what we are going through as loss, we will be better able to grieve and thus also be better able to get through the discernment process.

This conclusion is based on the following previously-stated presuppositions: Responding to call involves change; change involves loss; all significant loss gives rise to grief. The discernment process involves significant changes and losses and therefore grief. If we recognize and name the changes in the discernment process as loss, we will be better able to grieve those losses and thus better able to move through the discernment process toward acceptance of God's call. This chapter will develop particular aspects of these presuppositions.

Change involves loss

In chapter three *loss* was identified as the primary paradigm that encompasses grief and the grieving process, and includes loss due to death, as well as such losses as loss of health, wealth, and bodily functions. This framework has become standard in the 1990s, and most of us no longer think of death as the only type of loss. We are able now to recognize that significant change—of any type—involves loss, even when that change seems to be "for the better." So, for example, when we finally graduate after eight years of part-time theological study or four years of college, we view this graduation as loss as well as gain, as a time for grieving as well as a time for celebration.

Kathy was in her last semester of seminary and scheduled to graduate in a few months. She had been looking forward to graduation day for the last three years. The long commute had been difficult and the time spent on campus was disruptive to her home life. Her denomination was so short of ordained clergy where she lived that they were training laity to serve as lay pastors, although their preference was for theologically trained, ordained pastors. So her denomination was pleased to have another candidate about to graduate and be ordained. And she was pleased, too, or at least she used to be. This is what she felt called to do and what she had spent three years preparing to do. Why then did she feel so unhappy when thinking about graduation?

Her feelings of sadness isolated her from her classmates who all talked about graduation with great anticipation. She didn't share their enthusiasm and she felt she couldn't tell them of her reservations. When Kathy came to talk with me we were able to name the feelings she was experiencing as feelings related to loss: she would no longer be a student, a role she had enjoyed; she would no longer be a part of a seminary community where she experienced the support and encouragement of her peers; she would no longer have the freedom to go worship at whichever church she felt like on Sunday, or to sleep in if that is what she felt like doing. As she began to name all the changes she was experiencing and then to name those changes as losses, she felt her energy returning. For Kathy, naming graduation as loss as well as celebration freed her to experience her sad feelings as an acceptable part of the process. She found she was even able to share her sadness with a few friends. She discovered that some of them had also experienced similar feelings but had been afraid to tell anyone about them. She no longer felt alone in her feelings and no longer felt guilty for being sad. By graduation day, she had sufficiently named and grieved many of her losses so that she was able to enjoy and celebrate the day as she continued to grieve.

Any significant change will involve loss. When the change is one that we believe "everyone" thinks is a good one, we do not think we can say that the change is a difficult one for us. For instance, as we make preparations to marry, many of us believe that we are expected to talk about how happy we are and how much we are looking forward to married life. We may think that we have to hide any feelings of sadness, distress, uneasiness, or doubt. We may even think that our sadness is a sign that we are not in love with the person we are marrying. We may tell ourselves, "If I loved him, I would be happier." In acknowledging our sadness and looking to its source, we will be able to name the significant changes that are occurring and to recognize that these changes are losses that have evoked in us a grief reaction. We are experiencing the loss of being single, the independence of living on our own, the freedom of taking care of only ourselves; we may be experiencing the loss of our family name or of being a single parent or of living in the family home. By naming our changes as losses, we can grieve these losses and get through them so that we can also celebrate our new life.

Half the work of grieving is *naming* and *recognizing* that a loss has occurred or is occurring. Many of my students, clients, and friends have expressed enormous relief in being able to name what they are experiencing as grief.

Terry sat in my office, clearly struggling with words and with the feelings that were swirling within her. When I gently suggested that she had experienced a number of losses lately, her strained face softened, and she sighed. "Do you think I may be *grieving* then?" she asked tentatively. "It certainly seems that way to me," I responded. Her relief was palpable. It was as if a great weight had been lifted from her and things were okay now; *she* was okay now. "So, I guess I'm not crazy after all," she said. "No," I responded, "you are most definitely not crazy, but you are experiencing grief."

Much of Terry's "grief work" still needed to be done. She was "only" naming what she was experiencing. Yet so much of her energy went into worry about what it was that she was experiencing that naming the feelings as grief

marked an extraordinary step in the grieving process—
what I am calling "the halfway mark."

Loss needs to be named

How important is a name? Thomas Szasz (53) argued that
labeling people by various psychiatric diagnoses and calling
them mentally ill was done at the convenience of psychiatry and to the detriment of the person and her treatment.
This standardization failed to take into account that the
same illness might be treated differently in different situations. Whether we agree with Szasz's reasoning or not, we
are more likely to agree that the term "labeling" has a
negative connotation and the term "naming" has a much
more positive tone.[1] Thus in relation to the discernment
process, I have chosen to talk in terms of "naming" loss
and grief.

According to Samuel Rayan,

> A name is rarely, if ever, a simple label. It is not
> wholly true that a rose would smell as sweet by any
> other name. The concrete experience of a rose
> would, I imagine, differ from that of a gulab. A name
> not only denotes something, but also carries a wealth
> of connotations which it has acquired in the history
> of its usage.... Every name arises out of an encoun-
> ter between reality and people. It expresses a hu-
> man group's response to reality's self-disclosure in a
> given place and time. No name, then, may be
> looked upon as purely arbitrary, external and subjec-
> tive... (3-4).

Names describe, denote mystery and power, bless, liberate, harm, or are used for evil (Rayan 6-7). When we speak of naming the changes that occur in the discernment process as *loss* and naming our reaction to these losses as *grief*, we are speaking of no small task, no easy or frivolous process.

Paul Tournier points out that our name both distinguishes us from others, as well as unites us: "What separates and distinguishes me from other people is the fact that I am called by my name; but what unites with them is the very fact that they call me" (5). When we name our losses and our grief, we are both distinguishing our particular experiences and naming them. We are also uniting ourselves with everyone who experiences similar losses and who dares to name their losses and acknowledge their grief.

For the ancient Israelites, the uttering of the divine name was forbidden, "lest it should cause a dangerous discharge of power" (Rayan 6). Thus the Tetragrammaton YHWH in the Hebrew Scriptures symbolizes the unspeakable, unpronounceable name of God. In the Hebrew Scriptures only creatures have names; the Creator has none. Although in later centuries we have attributed many names to YHWH, it is really impossible to do so, for in doing so we are confining God in a definition or in a limited image (Tournier 24-25).

In Genesis 2:19 YHWH[2] charges the human being to give names to the animals, which are already in existence. In giving names to these creatures, the human being becomes *conscious* of their existence (Tournier 26). In this situation, the name exists for the benefit of the namer. This is also true of loss and grief in the discernment process.

74

Loss and grief exist whether we name them as such or not; we name them so we can gain consciousness of them. Just as the human being in Genesis gained power and mastery over the animals, while co-existing with them, we too are gaining power and mastery over our grief while we continue to live with our grief.

More recently we have struggled with what to call ourselves as various ethnic groups: am I white, Caucasian, or Euro-American? Black, Afro-American, or African-American? Hispanic, Mexican-American, Latino, or Chicana? We have found that we *can* name *ourselves* thus expressing our own identity, independence, pride and power as a people. *Who* does the naming is pivotal here. Likewise, by naming and acknowledging our own losses *ourselves*, rather than having them named *for* us, we empower ourselves to work through our grief.

All significant loss gives rise to grief

Discernment involves loss that needs to be named and then grieved. If we do not name and grieve the losses involved in discernment, we may not be able to fully respond to God's call.

Another way to state this is, if we recognize the changes that occur in the discernment process as "loss," we will be better able to grieve those losses and thus better able to move through the discernment process to the acceptance of God's call.

As we begin to acknowledge and respond to God's call, we are faced with both the challenges and the joys that process entails. Recognizing these challenges and joys helps us to move on. We do this by:

- encountering changes;

- recognizing which changes are losses; naming the changes as losses;

- identifying particular losses as obstacles; and

- getting through the losses by grieving them.

Encounter changes

Patricia knew that she was responding to God's call and that she was going through a process of discernment. She could acknowledge God's call and actively entered into the discernment process. In responding to God's call, however, she felt lost and disillusioned. She had sold her home, moved her family, given up her job, and started seminary. Why, then, she asked me, did she want to quit seminary and move back to where she came from? "I should be grateful," she told me one day. "I have a scholarship, my kids are happy here, and I'm doing well in my classes. Why, then, am I not happier, more content, and fulfilled? I thought I would feel at peace after coming here. Instead, I feel terrible, and I feel guilty for feeling so bad."

As we looked at all the changes in Patricia's life, what she left behind and what was lost to her, she began to see and then acknowledge that she had actually faced many changes in coming to seminary:

- She had given up a good paying job and was now making $5.00 per hour at a student job; money was tight.

- She had sold her home and was living in a small two-bedroom apartment.

- She had moved away from family and friends and didn't have any family nearby.

- She had moved away from her home congregation and pastor.

- She had moved from a medium-sized town in the South to a city in the Northeast.

- Her relationship with God had changed; she felt closer to God now, but she also felt accountable to God in a new and uncomfortable way.

Recognize which changes are losses; name the changes as losses

Once Patricia began to recognize that many of the changes in her life were also losses, she began to name them as such. She made a list of all the changes that occurred and put an asterisk in front of all the ones that might be called loss. Then she went through her list renaming the change as loss and stating it as such:

- Leaving my good paying job is a loss for me.

- Leaving and selling my house is a loss for me.

- Becoming a student is a loss for me.

- Leaving my church is a loss for me.

"Naming her demons" is how she described the process to me, then casting them out. Patricia wanted to get rid of them quickly. But she soon discovered that this would only be a temporary solution. It would mean going around the loss only to find herself confronted with the same demon or loss again. So she began to go through the losses one by one.

Identify particular losses as obstacles

Patricia took her list again and put exclamation points in front of those losses which she saw as obstacles in her discernment. At first she was tempted to put an exclamation point in front of all the losses because they all felt like obstacles. However, as she spent time with her list, she was able to see that some of her losses that seemed like obstacles were not. For instance, "leaving my church is a loss for me" seemed like an obstacle for Patricia; yet she found she had been able to connect with a warm, loving, and supportive congregation near the seminary. Although she grieved the loss of her home community, she would not name this loss as an obstacle. She did put an exclamation point in front of "leaving a good paying job is a loss for me." She was struggling financially with living expenses and tuition and found she might have to take a leave of absence from seminary so that she could raise some tuition money. (I will explore other types of obstacles in the discernment process in chapter five.)

Get through the losses by grieving them

This was difficult work for Patricia, as it is for most people. At first she felt she didn't have the time or energy to do this; but then she discovered that *not* doing this was taking up more of her time and energy. She decided to actively enter into "grief work"[3] or what I call *grieving* work.

I once was asked, "What do you mean by 'grieving work?'" "Doing grief work" is a phrase that is used often, and one I myself use frequently; but when I was asked the question, I realized the meaning may not be so obvious.

To *work* our way through grieving assumes that we have named an experience of significant loss and that we have "gotten through" the first "stage" of grieving. We are in the middle "stage" of disorganization and despair. Working through our grieving at this stage means that we continue to acknowledge loss *and* to *express* the emotions we feel in relation to this loss in forms appropriate to us. This may mean talking, yelling, crying, praying, spending time alone, journaling, or exercising, or any combination of these expressions. Psychologically, we need to "decathect"—to de-invest our emotional energy from the lost object, relationship, or person. Spiritually we need to spend time at the tomb, to live through Good Friday and Holy Saturday. We do this so that psychologically and spiritually we may eventually move on to the final stage of grieving—re-investing our emotions in a new object, relationship, or person. We do not celebrate the resurrection of the person, relationship, or object that was lost but our *own* internal resurrection. *We* are indeed alive again. We do this grief work on our own, but more often we do this grief work with the help of a friend, counselor, or spiritual guide.

To summarize, it is essential that we name the changes in the discernment process, identifying which changes are losses. This frees us to actively grieve these losses and to get through them. Getting through the losses enables us to be better able to hear our call and to go through the discernment process.

Chapter Five

Identify and Work Through Complications

S ome losses are more difficult or complicated than others because they evoke within us grief symptoms and reactions that are more intense and last longer than "ordinary" grief. These types of losses overwhelm the griever's ability to accept, to cope, and to move on, and leave the griever stuck in grief or unable to grieve.

There are two types of losses:[1] physical or tangible loss and psychosocial or symbolic loss (Rando, *Treatment of Complicated Mourning* 20, 26). *Physical losses*—the loss of a tangible object such as a car, a house, a breast, or a person (20)—can become complicated or difficult for a number of reasons. This is particularly so when the loss is the death of a person and the death is:

- sudden and unexpected (traumatic, violent, mutilating, random);

- from an overly lengthy illness,

- the death of a child, or

- when the mourner's perception is that the loss was preventable (5).

In addition to these factors, other factors can complicate the mourning of a person's death (5–6):

1. One's pre-death relationship with the deceased was very angry, ambivalent, or dependent.

2. The mourner has previous or current handicaps such as "unaccommodated" losses or stressors or mental health problems.

3. The mourner perceives a lack of social supports.

Rando specifically ties these complicating or high risk factors to the *death* of a loved one. I would suggest that some of the same factors could be complicators in other types of physical and even psychosocial losses such as losses that occur in the discernment process.

An alternative listing of complicating factors has been compiled by Froma Walsh and Monica McGoldrick. In general, the manner of death, the function of the family as a social network, the lifecycle timing of the loss, and the sociocultural context are potential complicating factors (25). Also, sudden or lingering deaths, ambiguous loss, and violent deaths are particularly difficult or complicated losses (13–16).

A more detailed, specific list is offered by Walsh and McGoldrick in relation to complicated factors in loss (25):

(a) sudden or lingering death

(b) ambiguous loss

(c) violent death, especially suicide

(d) enmeshed or disengaged family patterns, lacking tolerance for different responses or cohesion for mutual support

(e) lack of flexibility of system

(f) blocked communication and secrecy, myths, taboos surrounding death

(g) lack of kin, social and economic resources

(h) important role functioning of the member lost, with precipitous replacement or inability to reinvest

(i) conflicted or estranged relationship at death

(j) untimely loss

(k) multiple losses or other family stressors concurrent with loss

(l) multigenerational legacy of unresolved loss, particularly transgeneration anniversary reactions

(m) family belief system invoking blame, shame, or guilt surrounding death

(n) sociopolitical and historical context of death, fostering denial, stigma, or catastrophic fears

If a loss involves *any* of the factors listed by Rando or Walsh and McGoldrick, the resulting grieving may be more complicated—i.e., delayed, conflicted, chronic (Rando, *Treatment of Complicated Mourning* 61). Rando also notes that if even one of the "R" processes of mourning is compromised, the grieving may be complicated. These "R" processes of mourning are:

> recognize the loss...react to the separation...recollect and reexperience the deceased and the relationship...relinquish old attachments to the deceased

and the old assumptive world...readjust to move adaptively into the new world without forgetting the old...reinvest (45).

Although Walsh and McGoldrick have also linked their complicating factors particularly to loss due to death, I would suggest that these factors may be applicable to other types of loss. Rando supports this suggestion when she says that reactions from losses other than death

> may never reach the same intensity as reactions after the death of a beloved person, but they are variations on the same theme—psychological, behavioral, social, or physical reactions to the perception of death (26).

Other types of losses, or what Rando calls *psychosocial losses*, include losses such as divorce, chronic illness, death of a pet, and rejection from college (26). These losses can be complicated because of the presence of any of the complicating factors already listed, by any compromise or interference in the six R processes of mourning (45), or because these losses tend not to be acknowledged by others "as losses generating feelings that require processing" (20).

I have already argued that the discernment process involves a series of losses that need to be grieved. I have also stated that 50 percent of the grief work comes through awareness and naming of particular losses by the griever. Therefore, I would add that losses that occur during the discernment process can be complicated, not only by the failure of others to acknowledge or to recognize that a loss has occurred, but also because the discerner has failed to recognize that a loss has occurred.

In essence, some of the losses of the discernment process might be considered losses that result in "disenfranchised grief"—"the grief that persons experience when they incur a loss that is not or cannot be openly acknowledged, publicly mourned, or socially supported" (Doka 272). And when disenfranchised grief is present, emotional reactions are intensified (274) and become complicated.

I suggest that there are complications in the discernment process and concurrently the grieving process because of:

1. lack of awareness of a call

2. lack of understanding of a call

3. lack of acceptance of a call

4. lack of validation of a call

These four deficiencies, which can be distinct or can overlap considerably, are also accompanied by various complicating factors as delineated by Rando and Walsh and McGoldrick, leading to both complicated grieving and complicated discernment.

Complicated grieving due to lack of awareness and other complicating factors

One example of this type of complication in the discernment process which coincides with a complication in the first stage of the grieving process is a coming to awareness that a call has been issued or that a loss has occurred. This was described in my own discernment story (see Prelude). I could not believe what God was calling me to, and I could not name what I was experiencing as call or loss because I could not trust what I was experiencing. According to the Rando and Walsh and McGoldrick lists, the following complicating factors existed:

1. My previous relationship with the church was angry and ambivalent.

2. I had concurrent stressors in my life.

3. I perceived a lack of social acceptance and support.

4. The church system lacked tolerance for a different response.

5. The church was inflexible.

6. There was secrecy and taboos surrounding my experience.

7. I lacked church and economic support and resources.

8. I was experiencing multiple losses.

9. The church invoked shame, blame, and guilt surrounding my experience of call.

According to Rando and Walsh and McGoldrick, if even one of these factors is present, grief is more likely to be complicated. I have identified the presence of nine complicating factors in my discernment story. The most difficult of all the complicating factors was the negation of my call, which included a negation of my subsequent grief.

From the moment I first heard my call, my process of discernment and grief was predisposed to complications because of these factors and because of the denial on the part of my church that I had a call (see references in Prelude). Thus, if I had no call, I did not experience loss when my call could not be fulfilled. I would suggest that the church could remove a number of these complicating factors and will spend time in chapter six describing ways that this can be done.

Complicated grieving due to lack of understanding of a call

In my own story I focus on the example of a Roman Catholic female. However, we need not be Roman Catholic, or female to experience blocks, or complicating factors in our discernment process. Charles Myers relates the difficulties African-American women and men from various Protestant denominations have experienced in believing and being believed in their experience of call. When we cannot find another person to recognize or even believe our call, an *understanding* of our call is very difficult.

When we do not recognize or acknowledge another's call we are doing a disservice to that person, contributing to their confusion and to their losses, and we are also doing a disservice to God. Complicated grieving, such as what Roman Catholic women experience in relation to their call to the ordained priesthood, also causes our Creator to grieve.

I believe in a God who suffers with us and who cries with us in our grief. I believe that when women are prevented from living out their calls to the ordained priesthood, or when any one of us is prevented from hearing and understanding our call, God is as sorrowful as we are. When we prevent others from living out their call, we as individuals and as a community of faith contribute to the sorrow of our Creator.

Complicated grieving due to lack of acceptance of a call

Lack of acceptance of the call and resulting losses may come from the lack of acceptance of others or from the lack of acceptance of the discerner. When the lack of acceptance comes from others, we may doubt our call or may become confused, angry, disoriented, and unsure. Such was the case with Ellen who thought that she had a call to the priesthood. Her pastor did not question that she experienced a call, but he could not accept that it was a call to the priesthood since he believed "God does not call women to the priesthood." Ellen comes out of a Roman Catholic tradition. Her experience is similar to others of us whose church policy negates our call because of our gender or because we are openly gay.

My experience as a Roman Catholic woman was that, because of the teaching of my church, I did not even seek the acceptance of another person until many years after hearing my call. I could not recognize that I had a call for many years. Ellen, on the other hand, was *certain* of her call from the first moment and had no trouble understanding what God was asking of her.

Her complication developed when she brought her call to her pastor. He did not accept that her call was a call to the priesthood, and therefore he did not validate her call. This led Ellen to consider a number of possibilities:

- ignoring her call and staying in her church;

- leaving her church and joining another church that accepted her call;

- acknowledging that she had a call and finding an alternative way to live it out.

Ellen found that no matter which path she chose, she would face a number of losses: loss of living out her call and all that involved, or loss of her church community, family and friends, or loss of her certainty of purpose in following God's call. None of these paths sounded desirable for all these ways represented paths of complicated discernment and grieving due to a lack of acceptance.

Complicated grieving due to a lack of validation of a call

When I was finally able to "hear" my call, acknowledge it, understand what was being asked of me, and to accept that I had a call to the priesthood despite the opposition of my church, I continued to desire and look for further validation of my call. In clarifying my call I had cautiously and informally talked with others about whether or not women can be called to the priesthood, checking out their reactions and perspectives, reluctant to come right out and say that I believed that I had a call to ordained ministry. It was not until I was in college that I understood my call well enough to talk about it. To get to this point meant that I had already felt validated within my heart and believed I would be validated by the one I voiced my call to. Because of my internal certainty, I would have been confused, disappointed, and angered if I was not validated and would then have had to face the loss of support that I was counting on. I might even have lost the confidence to share my call with another person, afraid he or she too would not validate my call.

I actually found a number of *individuals* who validated and affirmed my call; however, *communal* validation eluded me. I looked for a statement from Rome acknowledging that I at least had a call; I looked to local Roman Catholic communities to affirm me and was disappointed on both fronts. It was not until I redefined what "community validation" meant that I was able to experience validation on a communal level. I can now count many "communities" among my validators as I no longer look to Rome as my primary community. My complication remains that because of a lack of a validation from the institutional Roman Catholic Church, I cannot live out my call. The good news is that I have been able to work through a number of the complications in the discernment process, to accept my call, and to be affirmed in my call.

Susan's story paralleled mine quite closely. She, too, felt a call to the priesthood. She too, was a Roman Catholic woman. After working through the first three complications (awareness, understanding, and self-acceptance), she found that she needed to have the institutional church support and validate her call. When she realized this was not going to happen in the near future, she sought her communal validation in the Episcopal Church, which welcomed her with open arms and validated her call from the beginning. After only a few years of additional training and formation she was ordained a priest and now serves as rector of one of the largest Episcopal churches in her diocese. Susan was able to get through her complications in discernment by leaving the Roman Catholic Church. Although her story has a happy ending, and she is happy with her decision, she has also had to grieve the losses of her former church community, friends, and original call to be a Roman Catholic priest.

The next chapter will address how we—as individuals and church—can correct many of the complications we unnecessarily place in the discernment processes of others. Before that, I will spend some time describing a few types of unresolved grief that may occur because of the complications present in a discernment process.

Types of unresolved grieving

In *Grief, Dying, and Death*, Rando lists seven types of unresolved grief that may occur because of complications in the grieving process (59–62). Four are particularly relevant to complicated discernment processes:[2]

1. absent grief—feelings of grief are absent, as if the loss has never occurred; there is a denial of the loss; we remain in a state of shock. We are caught in denial. It is in the working through of denial that anxiety decreases as fears are identified (Linns 26). When we get caught in this phase, we remain in a constant state of anxiety, unable to identify our fears. This would be typical of the discerner who denies or is denied a call.

2. delayed grief—grief is delayed up to years. The full grief reaction may be triggered by another loss or event related or unrelated to the original loss. This type of grief appears in older women who have put aside grief in order to raise children and take care of their family. Once the children are grown and out of the house we are able to recognize and grieve losses never previously addressed. These losses include the loss of pursuing our call to ministry. This is evidenced not only in the complicated grieving of Roman Catholic women who have been unable to acknowledge our call and our accompanying losses, but in the ordinary grieving of the many adults from various denominations who are entering seminary in their forties. They also grieve that they did not pursue their call earlier, but they are more able to work through their grief because they are able to fulfill their call *now*.

3. conflicted grief—an enhancement or distortion of one or more expressions of normal grief while other facets of grief are suppressed; examples include extreme anger and extreme guilt—both found to be especially evident in dependent or ambivalent relationships.

    The Linns claim that it is in the working through of our anger in our grieving that the fears that come from factors outside ourselves is decreased, and that anger not worked through results in depression (26). To be stuck in our anger is difficult and yet this is where many of us are indeed stuck in our grieving, particularly because of the love/hate, dependent/ambivalent relationship we have with our church. Likewise, fears coming from factors inside ourselves decrease as we work through guilt (26). When this does not happen and guilt remains predominant, so also do the fears that come from within. These extremes of anger and guilt keep us stuck in the grieving process and thus the discernment process, unable to get through to resolution and acceptance.

4. chronic grief—continued expression of intense grief that is really appropriate only in the early stages of loss; grieving fails to draw to its logical end. Many of the cases of complicated discernment that I have seen involve a distortion of anger or guilt (conflicted grief), and this remains the predominant type of unresolved grief in complicated discernment. If we are unable to work through our anger and guilt, we will probably be stuck in chronic grief, grief that knows no resolution because there is no logical end to the grieving. There is no transformation of the fears and anxieties, the anger and the guilt to what the Linns call "gift" (26). Thus conflicted grief, even when resolved, becomes not ordinary grief but chronic grief.

After describing the seven types of unresolved grief, Rando describes a number of therapeutic interventions that are especially appropriate for these types of grief (Rando, *Grief, Dying, and Death* 108-113). I have come up with an alternate list of "interventions" geared particularly to complications and unresolved grieving in the discernment process. These are described in chapter six.

Chapter Six

Become Better
Grief Guides

As a counselor I have seen that much of what brings people to counseling is unresolved grieving issues; many of us have never fully grieved our significant losses. This has prevented us from leading full and healthy lives, resolving issues, and moving on. I have witnessed the same phenomenon in my discernment work—both within my own discernment process and in my work with others. I have found that here, too, many of us get stuck in unnamed or unresolved grief. However, if we identify and name our losses, we will be better able to work through these losses and thus through our discernment process. Just naming what is going on as loss and grief is a beneficial step for many. Beyond this naming we must be able to grieve our losses in order to move forward both in our grieving process and in our discernment process. This will bring us closer to accepting God's call in our lives.

With a new-found awareness of our losses and an enhanced understanding of the grieving process including complications, we will be better able to help ourselves

95

through our grieving and discernment. Most of us, however, will still seek the guidance of others to help us through this process, especially if we are experiencing complicated or unresolved grieving and discernment. Seeking out guides—an individual, a discernment or grief group, and a community of faith—is a natural and necessary part of both the grieving and the discernment processes. This chapter, then, is written for those who desire to help *others* in their process. Obviously, however, these principles can also aid those who are reading this with their own discernment process in mind.

We can be better spiritual guides[1] to others by addressing the following six areas: attitudes, assessment, knowledge, skills, voice, and theology.

Attitudes

Those who wish to guide others in hearing and understanding God's call will benefit from nurturing certain attitudes. These include: respect, openness, flexibility, desire, perseverance, patience, genuineness, and gentleness.

Respect

Respect is a foundational attitude of acceptance. It is what Carl Rogers referred to as "unconditional positive regard" (283-284). It is valuing others simply because they are human beings. An attitude of respect allows us as guides to work with people who do and believe things that we disagree with and sometimes even abhor. In theological terms, an attitude of respect allows us to "love the sinner, hate the sin." If we do not have this most basic attitude of respect for those with whom we work, we will be unable to empathize with their stories. Respect assumes neutrality in the guide—an ability to hear a person's story without pre-judging actions or the outcome of the story.

Openness

Openness implies a willingness to allow new ideas, new thoughts, new feelings, and new experiences to occur within and among us. It involves a posture or a way of being that allows and even invites interaction, intervention, and dialogue. Openness involves trust and vulnerability and faith. Along with respect, it is one of the most foundational attitudes of spiritual guidance.

Flexibility

Flexibility is a partner of openness. Openness involves an ability to welcome new, unexpected, and even undesirable possibilities and experiences. When these experiences, ideas, thoughts, or calls come, it is flexibility that allows us to imagine different ways of responding. As guides we need to be flexible in the way we respond to those we are guiding. Flexibility assumes that there are a number of different ways to respond, and we will keep trying until we find the way(s) that are best.

Desire

Desire involves the inner core of our being, our heart's longing. Desire fuels our willingness to be open to another and to God. Desire is a necessary component of the discernment process. By desiring God's presence in our lives, we grow in our desire to know God's will for us. When we are in touch with our own desire for God, we are better able to help others to be in touch with *their* desire for God.

Perseverance

Perseverance is steadfastness and tenacity and is necessary particularly for those who work with discerners who face complicated discernment processes. The discernment process is a long and difficult one for many. An attitude of perseverance allows us to be willing to stay with the process and the discerner for the long-haul, to hold onto our belief that God calls everyone as we struggle to determine what a particular call means. This attitude of perseverance is a beneficial one to be nurtured in the discerner also, as it will be of great help when she faces rejection or when she is not supported or validated in her call.

Patience

Patience is tolerant endurance. Patience overlaps with perseverance. It is patience that underlies perseverance and allows guides to stay with discerners when they do not seem to be making progress in discerning. It is patience that gets guides through the most irritating, angry, and confusing moments in a guide relationship.

Genuineness

Genuineness means being ourselves as guides in the discernment process. To be genuine means to be real. It means that we will be honest and concrete in our responses; essentially this means that we will be human. We will show surprise and disappointment, excitement, and dismay. These are human emotions that we will not try to mask. Being genuine means owning our own feelings and responses without forcing them on another.

Gentleness

Gentleness is consideration and kindness. Gentleness is helpful to any guide, but especially for guides of discerners with complications in their discernment process. To be gentle means to be sensitive and have compassion for those we are guiding. Gentleness includes the understanding that guides challenge discerners with love and goodwill and with discerners' best interests in mind.

Assessment

Assessment in discernment involves the ability to identify changes, losses, griefs, and complications in the grieving and discernment processes. This ability to assess when loss has occurred, or when an obstacle is causing a complication, will allow guides to provide better guidance in discernment. It will also make guides more aware of limitations, revealing biases, inadequacies, and inabilities. This will allow guides to make referrals more readily. For instance, suppose we are able to assess that the discerner we are guiding is experiencing complicated discernment. The discernment is complicated due to lack of validation of a call, and this is exacerbated by a distortion in grief where extreme anger is present. In that case we should also be able to assess that we may need to refer the discerner to a counselor for help in working through her distorted grief.

By addressing and improving our assessment skills, we should also be better able to help a discerner determine whether a call is of God and the specifics of a call. This ability is enhanced by being part of a discernment group or community of faith.

Knowledge

As spiritual guides we need to know and understand as much as we can about the grieving and discernment processes and how they affect each other. This knowledge will:

1. give us a framework out of which to better understand discernment

2. allow us to recognize that changes may mean losses that need to be named and grieved

3. help us in assessing and intervening in situations of complicated or unresolved grieving and discernment, or knowing when referrals are necessary

4. give us additional cognitive understanding of discernment so as to be better equipped to provide guidance to another

Knowledge of the grieving and discernment processes will enhance our already existing knowledge as spiritual guides. This already existing knowledge includes familiarity with: different models of Christian spirituality, classical and contemporary writings in spirituality, and the Christian and the Hebrew Scriptures.

Voice

The ability to "hear" God's voice in our lives is foundational in coming to know how and where God is calling us. For some, this comes easily, for others unexpectedly, and for others, there is great confusion, doubt, and anxiety surrounding this first step in discernment. Chapter five has already detailed the reasons for complicated discernment, including obstacles in hearing God's call.

As guides and as church we need to examine how we contribute to a person's complications and difficulties in hearing God's call. We contribute to complications by:

- not fostering the eight previously described attitudes;

- diminishing or denying an individual's experience of call, and

- not having the necessary knowledge and skills to understand and intervene in complications in the discernment process.

In order for us to hear God, we must be able to hear ourselves and others. Since so much of difficult discernment is directly related to gender, it is necessary to give extra time and attention to our biases surrounding women. If we cannot listen to a discerner's experience of call because she is a woman, we are doing her a disservice. We are not allowing her to hear and clarify and understand what is between herself and God. We may remind her of a church policy that says she cannot fulfill her call in our church, but we are providing bad guidance if we do not allow her to fully *voice* her experience of call.

As guides we hear people tell us of experiences and activities which we do not agree with or condone; they also express beliefs that are contrary to our beliefs. However, it is not our right to stop them from telling their story. It is in the telling of the story that discerners gain clarity and insight, and it is only after the story has been told that we as guides can respond. Our responsibility as guides is to help discerners tell their stories and to help them make choices in regard to their stories.

In order for a discerner to tell her story, she needs to listen to God, certainly, but also to herself. According to Carol Gilligan, women, in particular, have difficulty in listening to themselves; women speak in a "different voice" which involves an ethic of care, a tie between relationship and responsibility, a different reality (173). It is incumbent upon us as spiritual guides to help each person find and hear his or her own voice, and then to articulate this voice to another.

Spiritual guides need to really listen to stories; we need to be able to encourage the telling and the articulation of these stories. To do this, we must first of all believe that these stories are worth telling and that they have validity. We must be willing to genuinely listen, for we all find our voice by telling our stories and being heard.

Skills

In order to listen to another, we first need to go back to using some basic listening skills. It is only when we are able to be present to and hear others that we can earn the right to challenge or to help them understand their story. Therefore, the most important skills we need to foster for ourselves as spiritual guides are the skills of attending, listening, and empathy, complemented by the ability to ask open-ended questions (probes). Only after we do this well and often should we move on to more advanced-level, challenging skills such as information sharing, self disclosure and advanced empathy (Egan) and reframing.

The basic skills

Attending—To attend to others means to be present to them physically, emotionally, socially, and spiritually. It means to be attuned to what is being said and how it is said. This requires of us, the listeners, a willingness to set aside or to at least acknowledge personal biases and filters, an ability to be focused and to focus on others, and a heartfelt desire to be receiving others' stories. This is the most basic of all counseling skills, yet it is rare to find someone who attends well.

Attending also involves attending to the context of the discerner and the guide relationship, paying attention to what factors and issues frame the relationship and the person, such as the factors of race, gender, issues of power, particularity of problem and morality (Patton 39-61). The guide needs to have an awareness of similarities and differences in the person's story and life and our own story and life, and be willing to look at how these intersections or separations affect us and the guide relationship.

Listening—Listening is a complex skill involving the ability to attend to another by attending to context, content, affect and meaning. There are a few negative types of listening that we need to avoid:[2]

1. Biased Listening—listening out of our personal beliefs (biases): Women should not be ordained; everyone should retire by the age of 65; God is female. We all have beliefs that can become biases. Some of these include thinking everyone holds the same beliefs we do, thinking we can hold our belief and still be open and present to another's story and perspective, or being unwilling to hear or accept the other person's story because it is different from what we believe.

2. Filtered Listening—listening done through particular filters. This is a lot like biased listening. Biased listening, however, prevents us from even hearing another's story. Filtered listening allows us to listen better, but we sort as we listen. We listen only to certain parts of a person's story while filtering out the parts we do not like or do not believe in or do not understand or do not approve of. Each person's filters will be different. As guides, we need to be aware of and name our filters and look at how they are preventing us from hearing another's story.

3. Evaluative Listening—a type of listening that is an extension of biased and filtered listening. As we listen, we evaluate the story as it is being told. In the most extreme form evaluative listening is judgmental listening; the guide judges what is being said and responds to what is said with evaluative, judgmental responses.

4. **Sympathetic Listening**—listening with sympathy for the discerner, instead of empathy. This involves feeling sorry for the other and comparing the story being told to elements of our own story without ever hearing the storyteller's perspective. Sympathetic listening is the antithesis of what needs to occur in a guide relationship.

Continuation of basic listening skills

Empathy—Empathic listening is the opposite of sympathetic listening; it means listening to a story from the other person's perspective, through the other's eyes. It is listening without judgment, evaluation, or bias. It is a moving beyond sympathy to empathy, walking in the other person's shoes, by first taking off our own. In empathy we listen for both the content of what a person says and the feeling behind the content.

Open-ended Questions (Probes)—This is the skill of asking questions that open up new areas of consideration. These are not informational or clarifying questions such as, "How old are you?" "Did you say you wanted to move?" Clarifying or informational questions are closed-ended questions that can be answered with a yes or no and are asked for the benefit of guides. Open-ended questions, or what Egan calls probes (121-126), open up new areas or new ideas for guides to consider and are asked for the benefit of the discerner, not for the benefit of guides. These questions encourage the discerner to broaden ideas and to consider alternative paths in her story. One caution is in order here. Although the discerner will often respond to an open-ended question with a response of "That's a good question; I never considered that," we as guides must not be tempted to continue asking question after question. As guides we need to sit with our questions for a while before we come up with another "good" one. Egan's rule is, after a probe, always respond with empathy before asking another probing question (126-127).

The advanced skills

Self-Disclosure—To self disclose means to share with the discerner some of our own story. The purpose of self disclosure is to benefit the discerner, not the guide. It is intended to be brief, and to the point, with the purpose of letting the discerner know that she is not alone, and with the purpose of serving as a model for her. Self disclosure is not done early in the relationship, as the focus of the early part of the relationship is on the discerner's story. Only after the discerner has been encouraged to tell her story, only after basic skills of counseling are used, and only after a relationship of trust and respect has been established, is self disclosure used.

Information Sharing—Information sharing is the sharing of appropriate and pertinent information with the discerner. This may mean sharing information about the discernment or grieving process itself. It may mean sharing information about resources for discernment, such as books, workshops, courses, or other information pertinent to an issue that emerges in the discerner's story. Information sharing needs to be closely connected to assessment. Sometimes it is sufficient to share with the discerner the stages of grieving so that she may understand what she is experiencing; however, if we as guides assess that the discerner is experiencing complicated grieving, we may need to go beyond information sharing about the grieving process to making a referral to a grief counselor. This act of referral also involves information sharing. We as guides will need to have a list of known and reputable counselors to share with the discerner.

Advanced Empathy—In using advanced empathy as a guide, we have read between and underneath the lines of what the discerner is saying, and looked at what is hinted at. We then form a hunch and use advanced empathy to check out our hunch. This skill is used only after we have established a good relationship with the discerner, only after we have heard a sufficient amount of her story to form a hunch and only after we have earned the right to do so by attentively and accurately listening to the discerner's story with basic empathy (Egan 182). The ability to read between the lines, to form hunches, and to see the broader picture, comes easily to some. However, a caution is warranted: we need to wait to use this skill. Most discerners do not want to be told too early what we are sensing about them or their story—whether that be an emotion or an idea. Discerners want to *first* be heard and understood from their own perspective.

Reframing through imaging

I use the skill of what I call reframing[3] by working with a discerner to identify and describe images or metaphors that correspond to the experiences she is describing to me. I often do this when I am getting lost in the discerner's words or when I sense that she is lost. I ask her for an image to describe what she has been saying, and then we work with whether this is an image of who or where she wants to be. Because it usually does *not* reflect who or where she wants to be, we work on *reframing* the image to reflect where she wants to be. For instance, if the image is that of a tight rope walker with a heavy load on one side of her pole that threatens to send her to her doom, we reframe her image to a tightrope walker with good balance and an equal load. As she becomes excited with her new image, we look at what is causing her to feel such a heavy load on one side of her pole and what needs to be done to balance her load. We use this image as a check-in at various points in our work; sometimes she may describe herself as that same tightrope walker afraid to even climb the pole and attempt to walk across the rope. Sometimes the discerner herself will want to reframe the image and come up with a new and more appropriate image. I find this often happens when I have supplied the initial image for her from what I am envisioning as she speaks. My preference is always for the discerner to come up with her own image; however, when she is unable to do so, I will begin an image for her, inviting and encouraging her to add to and change what I have imagined about her.

Theology

The guidance we are providing is *spiritual* guidance; good counseling or listening skills alone are not enough for us as spiritual guides. As spiritual guides we need to also be willing to address the profound faith questions that arise in the discernment process, which is also a grieving process. We need to do this in a "prophetic" way.

Theodicy: Why Me? Why does an all-good God allow suffering?

The most often-asked question in grieving and discernment is, "Why?" Why now? Why me? Why so much pain? Why must I suffer? Why did God do this to me? Why did God call me? These are questions asked out of our pain and our faith. They are questions we ask as grievers and discerners and questions we are asked as spiritual guides.

In relation to loss and grief as expressed as part of the discernment process, I have heard spiritual guides respond to these questions in a variety of ways:

- It's a mystery; we will come to understand in the life to come.

- I don't know, but I am willing to explore this with you.

- God never gives us more than we can handle; this is a test of your faith.

- Silence.

When these "why" questions are asked early on in the grieving and the discernment process, it is best *not* to answer, because at this point the griever is not so much looking for an answer as crying out in rage and pain (Mitchell and Anderson 171), and the discerner is not so much looking for an answer as expressing the depth of her spiritual experience. Any answer we give at this point will probably not be accepted by the discerner. Our role here is to *listen* to the pain and anguish of the discerner and to be *with* the discerner in his or her angst. These questions are also questions that come out of faith. As the discerner rails against God or questions God's purpose and wisdom, she is doing so out of an already existing relationship with God. If the discerner is allowed to express his or her feelings at this point, to feel *heard* by an earthly representative of God, and to be *encouraged* that God is a God who desires to hear anger, then the discerner will more likely be able to move on.

Later on, weeks or months after the loss has occurred and discernment has begun, the discerner may again ask, "Why?" This "why" comes out of the griever's terror and isolation. It is a plea not to be *abandoned* in the confusion of grieving and discerning. It demands from the spiritual guide *and* the community of faith continued presence, support, empathy, and caring, and an acceptance of a questioning of God's faithfulness (Mitchell and Anderson 171).

The discerner's fear is that she will be abandoned by God. The question becomes not only *why* do we suffer or *why* are we called, but *who* suffers with us, or *where* is God in our suffering (Mitchell and Anderson 171) and discernment? Spiritual guides can provide a ministry of *reassurance* here—that the discerner is not abandoned.

Finally, the discerner will once again ask why do I suffer? Why am I called? This time, the questions come even later on in discernment. The question now takes shape as: What are the *causes* of suffering, loss, and pain? And, how can the causes of suffering be modified or eliminated (Mitchell and Anderson 171)? When the discerner asks this question she *is* looking for a response from us. We as individual spiritual guides and members of discernment groups and communities of faith will need to have discovered our own theology of suffering and loss, and of differences between avoidable and unavoidable suffering.

Open and honest communication with God

This requires that the discerner be willing to both continue to "talk" to God, and to "listen" for God's presence in her life. One way that spiritual guides can encourage this type of communication is to introduce the discerner to a type of prayer called *lament,* which can be found in the Book of Psalms, and in the writings of various prophets. Lament is a type of prayer that extends out of an already existing relationship with God; it does not form the beginning of that relationship. Lament can be prayed individually or in the context of community. In lament, we first of all acknowledge our continuing relationship with God, and then we challenge God. In lament, we speak what is in our hearts—the positive and the negative—and we do so out of our pain, anger, and faith. In doing so we will often find that our grieving, healing, and discerning can begin.

> Theologically, [lament] is based on a belief that God will hear and must hear because it is the business of God to hear; psychologically [lament] is based on a belief that suffering people will not get help if they keep quiet (Karaban, *Isaiah* 30).

As spiritual guides, we can encourage that pain, anger, and questioning be expressed directly to God in prayers of lament; we can also be earthly reminder's of God's presence; and since the resolution of grief (and thus discernment [Karaban]) *requires* the presence of other persons (Mitchell and Anderson 107), we can provide through our human presence and our compassionate listening the opportunity for discerners to work through their discerning in the context of contemporary, caring communities of faith.

Remembering and hope

A main goal of grieving is to create a memory (Anderson, *What Consoles?* 377). We do this by *remembering*. We remember the person, the relationship, the good times and the bad, and we put together what Anderson refers to as an "emotional scrapbook" (377). In doing this we are opening ourselves both to grieving our loss and to creating a future. We remember so that we may keep a person or relationship alive in our hearts, and so that we can remember our past with the person or relationship, while acknowledging the absence. This is hard work at first and very painful. We *remember* the God of our childhood, our pre-discernment God, and put that image of God in our emotional scrapbook. The disciples had to follow a similar process. Following Jesus' death, his disciples and friends probably did not want to remember the last few days of his life. Yet it was in remembering these days—his suffering and death as well and his last meal with them—that the door was opened to a belief in his resurrection and his continued presence with us. We do this as part of our discernment process. We are working through our losses and our grief in order to better discern.

Remembering is closely tied to our ability to be hopeful (Anderson, *What Consoles?* 377). It is, as Henri Nouwen says, in finding "where our wounds most hurt" by *remembering*, that we will find consolation and comfort (16-17). I would add this is where we find *hope*. Not only do we need to remember what we lost, we also need to remember God's love for us. It is in the remembering of God's love for us that we as spiritual guides and communities of faith have a unique opportunity to minister to discerning individuals and communities. It is in the remembering of God's love that discerners have a unique opportunity to discern better. I call this opportunity prophetic.

It is a "prophetic perspective" that will allow us to go beyond our present-day, death-denying, death-defying, and grief-avoiding attitudes to an acceptance of death and grief as necessary and welcome parts of life and of the discernment process. It is the task of prophecy to draw out and nurture a consciousness alternative to the dominant perspective (Brueggemann, *The Prophetic Imagination* 13). It is a prophetic perspective that will call us beyond our individualistic approaches to grief ministry and discernment guidance to understanding that grief ministry and discernment guidance are part of the responsibility of *all* the members of communities of faith.

It is a prophetic perspective that calls us to acknowledge and accept our mortality as a gift from God and to understand that it is only in accepting our finitude that we are able to be complete (Mitchell and Anderson 173), and to complete our discernment.

A prophetic perspective requires of us a new language. It is a language of amazement and a language that captures our anguish. It is a language that overcomes the obstacles of bias, oppression, lack of flexibility and an unwillingness to validate another's call. It is a hope-filled language that cuts through our despair. The hope we have represents a "refusal to accept the reading of reality which is the majority opinion" or the institutional ruling; it is a hope that has "been denied and suppressed so deeply that we no longer know [it is] there" (Brueggemann, *The Prophetic Imagination* 67).

How do we resurrect this hopefulness? We do so through compassion and justice. To be compassionate means to move toward another when our inclination may be to move away, to be present with another as we struggle with our own pain, "in solidarity and community of experience." To be compassionate implies sensitivity and vulnerability and it requires that we take action against suffering and oppression (Hellwig 121). For Christians, it means to model our compassion on the compassion of Jesus—the incarnate compassion of God (127), who was able to enter into humanity—in all its aspects (123). For guides—individual, discernment groups, and communities of faith—to be compassionate, then, means to understand, listen, be present, risk, and act. To be compassionate means to suffer with the discerner, to enter into the human condition and the discernment process passionately and intimately. It means to convey our sympathy, and then our empathy to another hurting person, struggling in their discernment.

To take a prophetic perspective also involves the ability to act with justice. To feel compassion for another calls forth the accompanying value of justice, just as sympathy calls forth empathy. To be compassionate, or to love with justice, means to be able to allow God's gift of anger to flow in the cause of truth (Clarke 182). Love as compassion *must* be complemented by justice, for in compassion we desire to *be one* with the other; in justice, we desire the *otherness* of the other, and both are necessary for relationship

(180) and certainly, for guidance. Both compassion and justice are built on hope which is a commitment to direct our energy to rectifying conditions of those most loved by God (Falcone 11), the poor, the oppressed, the grieving, the discerning. Hopefulness, then, is resurrected by the *healing* that occurs when we are *reconnected* to others, God and self. We cannot resurrect hopefulness on our own.

To be prophetic requires us to resist our temptation to deny death and avoid the painful feelings of grieving. To be prophetic means to act out of justice and compassion grounded in faith and hope. This is a difficult call for all of us to heed, and we may often feel peripheral, lonely, and on the edges—much like the grieving feel. Yet it is a pivotal part of what we are called to do as we minister to the grieving and as we guide the discerner. We need to draw upon a prophetic sense of hope, compassion, and justice within ourselves while we also call upon that same sense of hopefulness, justice, and compassion in those to whom we minister and guide.

Postlude

Experiencing Resurrection

When I left for India In January 1984, I thought I was leaving my middle stage of grieving and entering the final stage of reintegration. I believed I had worked through my grieving by writing my dissertation. I was ready to let go, to move on.

Moving to India meant entering a new world and a new cultural and religious environment. We lived in a city of five million people where only a small percentage of people are Christian, and an even smaller percentage are Catholic. We lived on the campus of a large, Protestant seminary, and I entered into the religious practices of the campus. This meant attending weekly services which were in the tradition of the Church of South India, a unified church of Anglican, British Methodist, Presbyterian, and Congregational denominations. I occasionally made my way to a Roman Catholic Church, only to feel affirmed in my decision to put my involvement with the Roman Catholic Church behind me.

I soon discovered that there were nine Roman Catholic seminaries in the city we were living in, but none of them had female students or even female professors. Again, I felt affirmed in my decision and assured that I had moved on in my grieving and my discernment.

When we decided to return to the states, I applied to a number of Protestant seminaries, as I thought I was leaving behind my call to be a Roman Catholic priest or to even stay in the Roman Catholic Church. I interviewed at a number of large Protestant seminaries, only to find that I did not belong there. Finally, I received a notice about a teaching job at a small Roman Catholic graduate school that an acquaintance of mine thought would be perfect for me. She did not know of the recent developments in my discernment process. Since I was having no luck with the Protestant seminaries, I decided to pursue the advertisement. I applied, interviewed, and was immediately offered the job. These applications and interview processes transpired across twelve thousand miles and involved my flying from India to the United States and back, twice. It was quite an undertaking.

When I came to my present position I felt like I had come home. I had expected to meet with a number of angry Roman Catholic men and women—like those whom I had left behind. Instead, I found determined Catholics—clear on their calls to ministry and committed to staying in the Roman Catholic Church. I was challenged to open up my discernment process once again and to acknowledge and admit that my call remained to be a Roman Catholic priest and to minister within a Roman Catholic community. The call had never changed; it was I who had wavered.

I also found that although I had always seen teaching as what I was *allowed* to do, as an alternative to my call, I was very *good* at teaching, and felt at home there. I became involved with Women's Ordination Conference (WOC) as a way to continue my advocacy for women's ordination and discovered that I had new language to describe my call; it was indeed a call to the priesthood, but in the words of WOC, it was a call to a "renewed priestly ministry." These words freed me from trying to *reconcile* my ministry of teaching with my call to priesthood for it is my belief and hope that with a future, "renewed priestly ministry," I will have a clear choice whether to remain in teaching or whether to pursue my call to priesthood.

In my continued discernment I learned that the details of my call shifted as I remained open to continued conversations with God and continued discernment of how to live out my call in the present. I found much of my anger dissipating and transforming to actively renaming and reclaiming my call, my identity, and my sense of community. Community became those with whom I lived and worked and ministered, and to my delight, I found these groups of people affirmed me in my ministry. In short, I feel I was finally able to let go of much of the resentment, pain, and anger I had lived within for so much of my adult life and to experience the peace, happiness, and contentment of living out my call even though it was still only partially fulfilled. In grieving terms, I got through my grieving and reentered the world; in theological terms, I was reborn and experienced resurrection.

I can now say that I have accepted that my call to the priesthood is also a call to remain within the Roman Catholic tradition. Accepting this call, then, means being able to grieve the loss of fulfilling that call. What I have come to understand is that anyone's call to ministry will involve many losses. Some of us will experience additional obstacles that complicate our grieving and make our discernment more complicated, more compounded, and thus more continuous and harder to work through. Realizing this, however, has given me renewed energy and hope, both for myself and for others.

I continue to feel sadness because I cannot be ordained and fully live out my call. But I have sufficiently gone through the discernment process now to help *others* in their grieving and discernment. My responding to and living out my call now includes a supportive and affirming community that draws out from me my gifts of teaching, counseling, and guiding—without being officially, institutionally ordained. My responding to and living out my call now includes continuing to name and challenge the unjust structures that create and perpetuate complicated discerning and prevent those called by God to priesthood to live out that call. My responding to and living out my call continues to be to ease the sorrow of my Creator.

Endnotes

Introduction

1. See Prov 8:4, Is 45:4, Rom 8:28, 1 Cor 7:20, 2 Tim 1:9, Heb 3:1, and Eph 4:4 for examples of broad calls. See 1 Sam 3:3-10, Am 7:15, Ezek 2:2-3, Is 6:8-9, Jer 1:5, Acts 9, and Mk 1:16-20 for examples of specific calls.

2. These words come from the Roman Catholic "Rite of Baptism for Several Children" para. 62. This is the rite with which I am most familiar. Other Christian traditions use similar words. For example, see "Holy Baptism" 306 ("Through it [the water of baptism] we are reborn by the Holy Spirit") and "Baptism" w-2.3002 ("In Baptism, we die to what separates us from God and are raised to newness of life in Christ").

3. See also "Holy Baptism" 304-305. The priest asks those who are renewing their baptismal covenant to "continue in the apostles' teaching...persevere in resisting evil...proclaim by word and example the Good News of God in Christ...serve Christ in all persons...strive for justice and peace among all people." See also "Baptism" w-2.3006: "Baptism calls to repentance, to faithfulness, and to discipleship. Baptism gives the church its identity and commissions the church for ministry to the world."

Prelude

1. Myers would identify this as a call narrative because I am explaining my transformative experience in "retrospective interpretation" (7). I prefer to use the word "story."

2. Chapter three will describe these stages in detail.

3. Leon Festinger developed the concept of cognitive dissonance in 1957, defining this as a feeling of distress that occurs when two sets of beliefs fail to align (12).

4. See Sacred Congregation for the Doctrine of Faith's "Declaration," which clearly states that women are not called to the priesthood.

5. I still correspond with this man, Dr. Peter Beisheim of Stonehill College, North Easton, Mass., who continues to guide me through graduate school and beyond.

6. These stages of dying (with the addition of acceptance) were delineated by Elisabeth Kübler-Ross in *On Death and Dying*. According to Rando (*Grief, Dying, and Death* 27), these stages have also been applied to the grieving process.

7. My primary feeling of grief was anger, in which I felt stuck. The only way to get out of my anger and my grieving was to go *through* it. I am indebted to Carolyn Osiek (*Beyond Anger: On Being a Feminist in the Church*) for affirming this process and offering me new insights and perspectives.

Chapter One

1. All cases cited are composites, and the names used are pseudonyms.

2. See also Niebuhr et al., in which these dimensions of call are first referred to.

3. Wicks lists a total of ten resistances to prayer (104).

4. Turner and van Genep refer to this concept of "in betweeness" as a liminal or margin phase of passage. Myers refers to this "in betweeness" as a liminal or margin phase of call.

5. See Farnham et al., for a listing of conditions that *help* in discerning God's call: trust, listening, prayer, knowledge of Scripture, humility, discipline and perseverance, patience and urgency, perspective (30-35). Farnham et al. also suggest that *obstacles* arise from culture, prosperity, self-interest, self-absorption, self-righteousness, desire for security, desire for certainty, human time-frames and self-doubt (36-37).

6. See Cardinal Joseph Ratzinger's "Reply," which states that the Roman Catholic Church does not have the authority to confer priestly ordination on women, as presented in the Apostolic Letter of Pope John Paul II, *Ordinatio Sacerdotalis* (May 1994), and that this teaching is to be held definitively as belonging to the deposit of faith. On the positive side, the institutional church is no longer teaching that I cannot have a call but rather that the church has no authority to ordain me. My statement might seem to indicate that I accept this teaching. I do accept that a community of faith can choose not to ordain me, but not for the reasons stated in this letter.

Chapter Two

1. The emphasis here is on discernment of *call*; there are other decisions we can also discern.

2. See Au 127-128 for an eight-step model for discernment for novices in religious life: (1) Identify the decision to be made; (2) Examine the underlying values; (3) Pray; (4) Talk to a spiritual director; (5) Dialogue with the superior; (6) Strive for a state of Ignatian "indifference"—inner freedom and balance; (7) Accept superior's decision; (8) Stay open to continued experience for confirmation. See Fischer 114-128 for the following discernment guidelines for women:

1. Listen to your Deepest Self;

2. Affirm Your Own As Well As Others' Needs;

3. Do Not Confuse Passivity With Conformity to God's Will;

4. Trust the Insights That Come From Your Body, Intuition, and Feelings;

5. Be Aware of the Social and Cultural Forces Influencing a Situation;

6. Interpret Your Affective Experiences in Light Of Women's Social Conditioning;

7. Try to Generate Alternatives When You Feel Trapped;

8. Take Account of the Price of Change.

Fischer does the best job of anyone I have read in identifying the social and cultural obstacles faced by women in the discernment process; however, she stops short of naming the discernment process as a grieving process. See Rosage 158-161 for an eight-fold process for clarifying our discernment process: (1) Desire wholeheartedly God's preferences; (2) Clarify *what* we are discerning; (3) Beg God to reveal God's preference; (4) Seek other's advice; (5) Use our own talents in making our choice; (6) Meet with a spiritual director; (7) Consider negatives first, then the positives; (8) Make our choice only after being clear on what God's preference is for us.

3. See Wicks for a list of five key elements of daily mysticism; letting go and being in the now are the first two (39).

4. See Michael and Morrisey for a detailed look at what type of prayer is suitable for your particular personality type.

5. What I call contemplation and action Green calls discernment, "the meeting point of prayer and action in the life of the Christian apostle" (7).

6. The Holy Spirit produces good fruits of "love, joy, peace, patience, kindness, generosity, faithfulness, gentleness, and self-control" (Gal 5:22-23) ; the opposing spirit produces dissension,

bickering and immoral conduct (Gal 5:17-21). Other distinguishing fruits of the Holy Spirit are order and peace (1 Cor 14:32-33), freedom (Gal 4:12-31), unity (Eph 4:1-6), informed orthodoxy (1 Tim 1 :3-7; 2 Tim 3:1-9), thanksgiving and praise (Eph 5:18-20), kindness and forgiveness (Eph 4:30-32; 2 Cor 2:5-11).

7. Ramsey developed these ideas in a paper and is incorporating them into her M.A. thesis. I am thankful to her for sharing them with me.

Chapter Three

1. I am indebted to Mitchell and Anderson's book, *All Our Losses, All Our Griefs*, for first introducing me to this idea.

2. See Schulz and Alderman 137-147; Metzger; Mitchell and Anderson 84; Sunderland 34; Kastenbaum 14; and Feifel 24.

3. See Lindemann; Engel; Kübler-Ross 38-137; Bowlby 85; Tatelbaum 25-47; Rando, *Grief, Dying, and Death* 23-36; and Staudacher 4-7.

4. See Rando, *Grief, Dying, and Death* 36 and Rando, *Treatment of Complicated Mourning* 38 for fuller lists of physical or somatic manifestations of grief.

5. Bowen calls this feeling an "emotional shock wave," aftershocks of pain and grief that occur in the family system months and years after a loss has occurred (83).

Chapter Four

1. An exception to this is found in Rando, *Treatment of Complicated Mourning* 26. Rando uses "label" in positive terms in relation to grief when she says, "Merely having a label or a cognitive framework for distress...allows human beings to manage more effectively." Despite this positive reference, I prefer to use the term "naming" in relation to loss and grief.

2. A sampling of other scriptural references that denote the importance of names/naming include: Is 49:1, 2 Sam 12:28, Ps 49:11, Ex 2:10, 1 Sam 1:20, Acts 4:10-12, Mt 18:20 and Jn 20:16.

3. Lindemann coined the phrase "grief work" in 1944, noting that it takes *work* to realize and accept the loss of a loved one.

Chapter Five

1. In chapter three I refer to Mitchell and Anderson's schema of six types of losses; these six types of losses may be subsumed under the more general classification of Rando's physical and symbolic; types 1, 4, and sometimes 2 fall under physical losses, and 3, 5, 6, and sometimes 2 fall under symbolic losses. To simplify the ensuing discussion on complicated grieving, which refers often to Rando's work, I have switched over to her language of classification.

2. The three not described in this chapter are inhibited grief, unanticipated grief, and abbreviated grief. In *Treatment of Complicated Mourning,* Rando describes seven syndromes of complicated mourning: absent mourning, delayed mourning, inhibited mourning, distorted mourning, conflicted mourning, unanticipated mourning, and chronic mourning (154-183). I have chosen to use her earlier schema.

Chapter Six

1. Various terms are used for those who help discerners with their discernment process: spiritual directors, co-discerners, spiritual guides, soul friends, and pastors. I prefer the term spiritual guides.

2. Egan (100-103) lists a number of obstacles and distractions in listening: inadequate listening, evaluative listening, labels as filters, fact-centered rather than person-centered listening, re-

hearsing, sympathetic listening, and interrupting. I have short-
ened and revised this list.

3. Reframing is a process described by Donald Capps, who
builds on the work of Watzlowick, Weakland, and Fisch. I am
not using his definition of reframing.

Bibliography

Aleshire, D. O. "What Should Pastoral Identity and Pastoral Calling Mean?" *Journal of Supervision and Training in Ministry* 16 (1995): 22-28.

Anderson, H. "What Consoles?" *Sewanee Theological Review* 36, no. 3 (1993): 374-384.

———. "Forming a Pastoral Habitus: A Rich Tapestry with Many Threads." *Journal of Supervision and Training in Ministry* 15 (1994): 231-242.

Au, W. *By Way of the Heart.* New York: Paulist Press, 1989.

"Baptism." In *The Constitution of the Presbyterian Church (U.S.A.) Part II: Book of Order*, w-2.3000–w-2.23014. Louisville: The Office of the General Assembly, 1995.

Bausch, W. J. *Storytelling: Imagination and Faith.* Mystic, Conn.: Twenty-Third Publications, 1984.

Bowen, M. "Family Reaction to Death." In *Living Beyond Loss: Death in the Family*, edited by F. Walsh and M. McGoldrick, 79-92. New York: W.W. Norton & Co., 1991.

Bowlby, J. *Attachment and Loss: Loss, Sadness and Depression.* Vol. 3. New York: Basic Books, 1980.

Brueggemann, W. *Living Toward a Vision.* Philadelphia: United Church Press, 1976.

————. *The Prophetic Imagination*. Philadelphia: The Fortress Press, 1978.

Capps, D. *Reframing: A New Method in Pastoral Care*. Minneapolis: Augsburg Fortress, 1990.

Carr, Anne. "On Feminist Spirituality." In *Women's Spirituality: Resources for Christian Development*, edited by J. W. Conn, 49-58. New York: Paulist Press, 1986.

Clarke, T. E. "One Road to Peace: Tender Love, Firm Justice." *The Way* 22 (1982): 175-183.

Doka, K. "Disenfranchised Grief." In *The Path Ahead: Readings in Death and Dying*, edited by L. A. DeSpelder and A. L. Strickland, 271-275. Mountain View, Calif.: Mayfield Pub. Co.

Doohan, L. *The Lay-Centered Church: Theology and Spirituality*. Minneapolis: Winston Press, 1984.

Duraisingh, D. "Spirituality As the Directionality of Christian Living: Some Reflections." *Masihi Sevak* 10 (1984): 3-11.

Dussell, E. "Discernment: A Question of Orthodoxy or Orthopraxy." In *Discernment of the Spirit and of Spirits*, edited by C. Floristan and C. Duquoc, 47-60. New York: Seabury Press, 1979.

Egan, Gerard. *The Skilled Helper*. Pacific Grove, Calif.: Brooks/Cole Pub. Co., 1994.

Engel, G. "Grief and Grieving." *American Journal of Nursing* 64 (1964): 93-98.

Falcone. S. A. "Orientations on Four Theological Values Relating to 'Pastoral Circle' Model of Discernment." Unpublished manuscript used for integrative seminar class. Rochester, New York: St. Bernard's Institute, 1995.

Farnham, S. G., J. P. Gill, R. T. McLean, and S. M. Ward. *Listening Hearts: Discerning Call in Community*. Harrisburg: Morehouse Pub., 1991.

Feifel, H. "Psychology and Death: Meaningful Recovery." In *The Path Ahead: Readings in Death and Dying*, edited by L. A. DeSpelder and A. L. Strickland, 19-28. Mountain View, Calif.: Mayfield Pub. Co., 1995.

Festinger, L. *A Theory of Cognitive Dissonance*. Stanford: University Press, 1957.

Finley, J. *The Awakening Call: Fostering Intimacy with God*. Notre Dame: Ave Maria Press, 1984.

Fischer, K. *Women at the Well: Feminist Perspectives on Spiritual Direction*. New York: Paulist Press, 1988.

Gilligan C. *In a Different Voice: Psychological Theory and Women's Development*. Cambridge, Mass.: Harvard University Press, 1982.

Green, T. H. *Weeds Among the Wheat: Discernment: Where Prayer and Action Meet*. Notre Dame: Ave Maria Press, 1984.

Hammarskjöld, D. *Markings*. New York: Alfred A. Knopf, 1964.

Hart, T. N. *The Art of Christian Listening*. New York: Paulist Press, 1980.

Hellwig, M. K. *Jesus: The Compassion of God*. Wilmington, Del.: Michael Glazier, 1983.

"Holy Baptism." In *The Book of Common Prayer of the Episcopal Church*, 296-314. New York: The Church Hymnal Corporation, 1979.

Johnson, L. T. *Scripture and Discernment: Decision Making in the Church*. Nashville: Abingdon Press, 1983.

Karaban, R. A. "Pastoral Counselor: Role or Function? A Study of Pastoral Counseling and Pastoring in the Roman Catholic Tradition." PhD diss., Graduate Theological Union, 1983.

―――. "Isaiah 63:16–64:12: Pastoral Implications." *Lectionary Homiletics* 4 (1993): 29-30.

Kastenbaum, R. "Reconstructing Death in Postmodern Society." In *The Path Ahead: Readings in Death and Dying*, edited by L. A. DeSpelder and A. L. Strickland, 7–18. Mountain View, Calif.: Mayfield Pub. Co., 1995.

Kelsey, M. *Discernment: A Study in Ecstasy and Evil*. New York: Paulist Press, 1978.

Kübler-Ross, E. *On Death and Dying*. New York: Macmillan, 1969.

Larkin, E. *Silent Presence: Discernment As Process and Problem*. Denville, N.J.: Dimension Books, 1981.

Lindemann, E. "Symptomatology and Management of Acute Grief." *American Journal of Psychiatry* 101 (1944): 141-148.

Linn, M., and D. Linn. *Healing Life's Hurts: Healing Memories Through Five Stages of Forgiveness*. New York: Paulist Press, 1978.

McMakin, J., and R. Nary. *Doorways to Christian Growth*. Minneapolis: Winston Press, 1984.

Metzger, A. M. "A Q-methodological Study of the Kübler-Ross Stage Theory." *Omega* 10 (1979): 291-302.

Michael, C. P., and M. C. Morrissey. *Prayer and Temperament: Different Prayer Types for Different Personality Types*. Charlottesville, Va.: Open Door, 1984.

Mitchell, K. R., and H. Anderson. *All Our Losses, All Our Griefs: Resources for Pastoral Care*. Philadelphia: Westminster Press, 1983.

Mueller, J. *Faithful Listening: Discernment in Everyday Life.* Kansas City, Mo.: Sheed and Ward, 1996.

Myers, W. H. *God's Yes Was Louder Than My No: Rethinking the African American Call to Ministry.* Grand Rapids: William B. Eerdmans Pub. Co., 1994.

Niebuhr, H. R., D. D. Williams, and J. M. Gustafson. *The Purpose of The Church and Its Ministry.* New York: Harper and Row, 1956.

Nouwen. H. J. M. *A Letter of Consolation.* San Francisco: Harper and Row, 1982.

"The Ordained Ministry." In *The Book of Discipline of the United Methodist Church*, para. 401-457. 88th edition. Nashville: The United Methodist Publishing House, 1988.

Osiek, C. *Beyond Anger: On Being a Feminist in the Church.* New York: Paulist Press, 1986.

Palmer, P. *The Active Life: Wisdom for Work, Creativity and Caring.* San Francisco: Harper and Row, 1990.

Patton. J. *Pastoral Care in Context: An Introduction to Pastoral Care.* Louisville: Westminster/John Knox, 1993.

Premnath, D. N. "Spiritual Growth and Global Vision: The Experience and Sharing of Cultural Variation." Talk given at St. Bernard's Institute (with R. Karaban), November 21, 1988.

Ramsey, L. S. "Discernment in Community: A Liberating Process of Dis-illusioning, Resistance & Imagining." Unpublished paper, May, 1996.

Rando, T. A. *Grief, Dying, and Death.* Champaign: Research Press Co., 1984.

———. *Treatment of Complicated Mourning.* Champaign: Research Press Co., 1993.

Ratzinger, J. "Reply to the *Dubium* Concerning the Teaching Contained in The Apostolic Letter *Ordinatio Sacerdotalis.*" Vatican City: Congregation for the Doctrine of the Faith, 1995.

Rayan. S. "Naming the Unnamable." In *Naming God*, edited by Robert P. Scharlemann, 3-28. New York: Paragon House, 1985.

"Rite of Baptism for Several Children." In *The Rites of The Roman Catholic Church*. Vol. 1. Para. 32-71. New York: Pueblo Pub. Co., 1969.

Rogers, C. *On Becoming a Person*. Boston: Houghton Mifflin Co., 1961.

Rosage, D. E. *Beginning Spiritual Direction*. Ann Arbor, Mich.: Servant Pub., 1994.

Sacred Congregation for the Doctrine of the Faith. "Declaration on the Consideration of Ordination of Women to the Ministerial Priesthood." Vatican City, January 27, 1976.

Schulz, R., and D. Alderman. "Clinical Research and the Stages of Dying." *Omega* 5 (1974): 137-147.

Staudacher, C. *Beyond Grief: A Guide for Recovering from the Death of a Loved One*. Oakland, Calif.: New Harbinger Pub., Inc., 1987.

Sullender, R. S. "Three Theoretical Approaches to Grief." *The Journal of Pastoral Care* (December 1979): 243-251.

Sunderland, R. *Getting Through Grief: Caregiving by Congregations*. Nashville: Abingdon Press, 1993.

Szasz, T. S. *The Myth of Mental Illness*. New York: Harper and Row, 1961.

Tatelbaum, J. *The Courage to Grieve*. New York: Harper and Row, 1980.

Tournier, P. *The Naming of Persons*. New York: Harper and Row, 1975.

Turner, V. *The Forest of Symbols: Aspects of Ndembu Ritual*. Ithaca: Cornell University Press, 1961.

Van den Blink, A. J. Talk given at "Resourcing the Spirit" workshop. Rochester, New York, October 4, 1994.

Van Genep, A. *The Rites of Passage*. Chicago: The University of Chicago Press, 1960.

Walsh, F., and M. McGoldrick, eds. *Living Beyond Loss: Death in the Family*. New York: W.W. Norton & Co., 1991.

Wicks, R. *Seeds of Sensitivity: Deepening Your Spiritual Life*. Notre Dame: Ave Maria Press, 1995.

Wiesel, E. *Night*. New York: Avon, 1958.

Additional Discernment Resources

EXTRAORDINARY PREACHING
20 Homilies by Roman Catholic Women
Roslyn Karaban and Deni Mack

ISBN 0-89390-390-6, 96 pages, 5.5" x 8.5"

You don't have to be ordained to be invited to preach. You just have to be good. The women who gave the sermons in *Extraordinary Preaching* are good — and in demand. At retreat houses. At priestless parishes. At interdenominational chapels. At memorial services and weddings. People want to know where they are preaching next. Their homilies are concrete and colorful. They link the Scripture stories with the blood, bones, and dirty dishes of ordinary life. And they have various personal styles — from academic, to pastoral, to storytelling. These homilies will inspire you and show you what can be done from any pulpit.

AT-HOME MOTHERHOOD: Making It Work for You
Cindy Tolliver

ISBN 0-89390-295-0, 152 pages, 6" x 9"

This book validates your choice as an at-home mother and guides you toward exploring relationships, handling practical matters, and continuing self-development. Read this book and feel comfortable about your choices.

BALANCING YOUR LIFE: Setting Personal Goals
Paul Stevens

ISBN: 0-89390-375-2, 96 pages, 4.25" X 7"

The key to improving your life, according to noted "worklife" expert Paul Stevens, is planning. All you need is privacy, peace and quiet, a pad of paper, and lots of enthusiasm. *Balancing Your Life: Setting Personal Goals* provides that extra push. It will help you sort through the conflicting issues you deal with each day, the opportunities you want to explore, and the actions you need to take to bring balance to your life. In the end, you will emerge with a set of clear personal goals that will put you in charge of your dreams.

Order these books from your local bookseller or call: CODE: MQ
1-888-273-7782 (toll free) or 1-408-286-8505
or visit the web site at www.rpinet.com